The Management of Marketing

Other titles from Marketing Improvements Group Plc

How to Handle Major Customers Profitably

How to Recruit and Select Successful Salesmen

The Management of Marketing

Managing a Sales Force

Managing Sales and Marketing Training

Marketing Planning for the Pharmaceutical Industry

Motivating your Sales Force

Negotiating Profitable Sales

Organising for Improved Sales Effectiveness

Running an Effective Sales Office

Training Salesmen on the Job

Sales Management Handbook

SalesPlanner

20 Activities for Developing Sales Effectiveness

AUDIO MANUALS

Counselling for Poor Sales Performance

Making Effective Presentations

The Sales Presentation

Using the Telephone in Selling

The Management of Marketing

Mike Wilson

of Marketing Improvements Group Plc

Second edition

Wildwood House

First edition published in hardback 1980 by
Gower Publishing Company Limited

This second edition published in 1989 paperback by
Wildwood House Limited
Gower House,
Croft Road,
Aldershot,
Hampshire GU11 3HR,
England

Gower Publishing Company
Old Post Road
Brookfield
Vermont 05036
USA

British Library Cataloguing in Publication Data
Wilson, M.T. (Michael Thomas),
   The management of marketing.—2nd ed.
   1. Marketing
   I. Title
   658.8
ISBN 0–7045–06092

Printed and bound in Great Britain at
The Camelot Press Ltd, Southampton

For Simon, Vicky and Emmeline
who make it all worth while

Contents

Illustrations

Tables

Figures

Preface

When the possibility of a paperback edition of this book was first suggested, I viewed the prospect with a mixture of pleasure and trepidation.

I was pleased that, because of the differences in pricing and distribution, the book would be made available to a much larger audience than is accessible to a hardback publications. However, I felt concerned about how much of the original work was still relevant as it is some years since I completed the original manuscript and it is obvious that the world of business in general, and perhaps marketing in particular, is in a constant state of flux. In fact, one of the main reasons that the book was written in the first place was to help readers recognize and cope with the volatile world in which they lived then.

It was thus no easy decision to agree to this paperback edition. As a book buyer myself, I know how irritating it is to purchase an apparently new volune only to discover (usually too late) that it is an old out-of-date work in glossy new packaging.

As I reviewed this opportunity to re-publish however, I was encouraged by two powerful facts. First, that the original hardback edition is still being bought in quantity, often by our clients who comment on its continuing value. Second, as I am still in close contact with business through my work as a marketing consultant I felt confident that I could decide which parts needed eliminating or updating and which themes remained relevant.

Having reviewed the book in depth and pondered long and hard, I realized that although the nature and direction of many economic, political, social and technological forces had changed, the process and speed of such changes was still creating problems (and opportunities) for an increasing number of organizations. Thus the objective of the book, to help such managements effectively plan, organize and control their marketing processes within a dynamic environment, still remains valid, although the chapter on that environment 'Marketing in a Changing World' has had to be expanded and various other sections updated.

Further evidence of the continuing relevance of a book on how to plan and implement marketing activity came from the ever-growing body of analysis and research that has and is providing fresh insights into what makes successful companies successful. Starting with Peters and Water-man's seminal work *In Search of Excellence* through *The Winning Streak* (Goldsmith and Clutterbuck), Peters' further work *The Pursuit of Excellence*, McBurnie and Clutterbuck's *The Marketing Edge* and many others, there has been a steady flow of publications aimed at identifying the key characteristics of effective organizations. The common marketing conclusions from all of this research are interestingly very basic. That successful companies spend a great deal of time and effort in getting and remaining close to their customers, in creating customer-value driven cultures and organizations, in providing consistently high levels of customer service should not come as a surprise to most experienced managers.

The fact that these fundamental tenets need re-emphasizing suggests that the central issue of marketing remains implementation rather than one of concept or technique. This strengthens my view that a text on the management of marketing can still be of value as companies strive to make marketing happen.

Why this book?

This book is concerned with what might be called the 'implementation' phase in the evolution of marketing. This stage seems to be causing many difficulties and problems for a large number of organizations throughout the world and is likely to cause even more as an increasing number of companies (and countries) are forced to realize that professional expertise in the various tactics of marketing does not of itself guarantee success. It has been written because much of the existing literature tends to cover the techniques of marketing. Thus there are dozens of books on research, pricing, advertising, etc., either as individual subjects or as part of a treatment of the full range of marketing tactics. There seems to be little available which looks at the managerial dimension, and assuming that the reader is already knowledgeable about the basic marketing elements, discusses how best they can be planned, organized and controlled in a practical, systematic and profitable way. There are, of course, many texts on management and its various functions, but so often these are of a general nature and do not address the particular problems of top marketing management in a changing world. It is the primary objective of this book, therefore, to provide an up-to-date basis for the systematic review and improvement of the direction and management of the marketing activity.

Origin, content and usage

The content of the book is based on my experiences over the last twenty five years as a marketing consultant and management trainer. During this period I have had the unusual privilege of observing and working with many hundreds of organizations covering the whole spectrum of industry and commerce from fast-moving and durable consumer goods through industrial consumables and capital equipment to services marketing. These organizations have varied in size from large multinationals to small local firms, and in nature from private enterprise through trade associations to nationalized industry and government departments. My work with these clients has taken place throughout Britain and Western Europe, North and South America, Africa, Asia and Australia. During the same period I have also been involved in the creation and expansion of my own company which has grown from its inception in 1964 into one of the largest specialist marketing consultancies in Europe. This has meant that not only have my own findings and observations as a consultant been vastly augmented and refined by the work of my colleagues in Marketing Improvements, but also we have had to attempt to practise personally what is preached in the book in terms of directing and managing an organization marketing at home and abroad.

This book, then, is a crystallization of our experiences as consultants to others and as directors and managers of a commercial enterprise operating internationally. This combination of experience, supplemented where appropriate from the research and findings of others, has produced what I hope is a practical text of value to practising management. This emphasis on practicality is a major theme because so many senior managers seem to find much of the existing literature out of touch with reality. Although for the student or the academic it is perfectly justifiable to analyse marketing problems in the vacuum of the case study, the operating senior executive seeks help with life as it really is. He knows from his experience that the situations he is faced with are dynamic, that accurate information is hard to obtain, that manpower, money and particularly time, are very scarce, and worst of all, that short-term pressures always seem more urgent than planning the future. As one general manager put it, 'in this company we are so busy baling out the boat, we don't have time to stop up the holes'.

How can top management improve performance in this environment? It is our experience that first there must be a determination to concentrate the limited time available on the few key issues of the business.

If a company is to be successful, it must find answers to three fundamental questions:

Where are we now?
Where do we want to go?
How will we get there?

The fact that such questions seem naive and obvious should not blind management to the need to answer them; furthermore, although the questions may be simple, unfortunately the answers seldom are! In our experience unless clear answers are found (and of course, the answers can and do change in a dynamic world), it is virtually impossible to manage a company successfully. Those organizations that do not have solutions (usually because they are too busy to ponder the questions) tend to drift along, their long-term future simply an endless repetition of their short-term past, until they become out of touch with their basic purpose of satisfying consumer needs at a profit. At this point, they run into severe financial problems from which many never recover.

This glimpse of what should be the obvious fact, that it is management's prime responsibility to run the business, rather than allow the business to run them, is another emphasis of this book, and the reason why the content has been structured around the three questions listed above.

Each question is examined in some detail to try to identify what it means in reality.

The various stages of the marketing activity where the questions need to be put are identified and approaches to their resolution described. Examples are given wherever possible, most of them drawn from our recent consulting experience and therefore quoted anonymously. Finally, checklists are provided to try to bridge the gap between the reading of the book and, the most important task, the translation of it into practice.

This is not a marketing textbook in the normal sense of the word, because it does not give a complete description of all the methods and techniques involved in the various marketing tactics. Professor Kotler and many others have already done that far better than I could; for those readers who want a more complete coverage of any aspect of the marketing function, a booklist is provided. This book is more a philosophy of approach to business in general and marketing in particular, demonstrating a systematic and practical review process and highlighting the factors which seem to us important and which generally have not been covered in other writings. Its intention is to stimulate the reader to reflect more deeply on his own company's activities, to ask himself, his colleagues and his subordinates, the kinds of questions that are posed here and thus to develop further his own awareness, concepts and methodology.

Of course, the justification for a business book must be in terms of its practical application and effectiveness in improving results, however specified. To this end, it is suggested that the checklists should be used, not simply to reflect on the content of each chapter, but as review tools within the organization. They can and have been used by us as audit guides, as structures for reports, and as agendas for senior management workshops and meetings, leading to practical decision making. To facilitate such usage and to provide a complete overview, all the checklists from the end of each chapter have been repeated within a total model of the marketing function in 'A Systematic Programme for Reviewing and Improving Your Marketing Activity' beginning on page 154.

Who the book is for

This book is intended for those who are concerned with the direction and management of the marketing activity – which will usually mean the Marketing Director or Marketing Manager. However, it is hoped that it will be of value to the whole top management team, especially General

Managers and Managing Directors who, after all, must and do take a large share of responsibility for the marketing direction of their companies. Furthermore, it should be of interest to those currently in middle management who aspire to the top, and help equip them for their future roles. To provide a continuity of focus, it is addressed primarily to Marketing Directors in manufacturing companies, although most of what is said is equally applicable to the service and distributive industries; examples from such organizations occur from time to time as reminders of the universality of corporate problems!

Conclusion

The task which faces top marketing management today has paradoxically been made more difficult in some ways by the widespread acceptance of marketing techniques. Whereas in the production-oriented country of the blind, the one-eyed marketing company could be king, in a world of virtually universal vision, such simple advantages have disappeared.

In the future it will become increasingly difficult for any company to develop and maintain over a significant period major product or price advantages, uniqueness of marketing or sales skills, captive distribution or protected markets. Developments in education, communication, legislation, social attitudes and global economics and trading are together creating an environment where the competition for markets, distribution, staff and finance is increasing dramatically. We have already seen, throughout industry, companies disappear into bankruptcy or takeover as a result of this highly competitive international situation. Motor cycles, domestic appliances and textiles are but three examples of British industries that have been reduced or eliminated.

To prosper, even to survive, is thus becoming harder. This is why the 'management' phase of marketing evolution is going to be critical; given the increased competitive situation on the one hand and the difficulty of maintaining traditional advantages of products, prices or market allegiance on the other, it is the quality of the direction and management of the marketing activity which will make the difference between success and failure.

It is no easy task and there are no easy or universal solutions. Working with so many companies trying to plot their paths into the future has given us some indication of the preparation required today if tomorrow is to be successful. More than anything else, however, it has caused us to realize that though many routes may be wrong, there is no guaranteed right road. Thus it is with some humility and apprehension that I write this book, but also in the hope that these observations based on the practices of many successful companies (as well as unsuccessful ones) will be helpful to those readers faced with similar problems and opportunities as they lead their organizations into the ever more complex future.

For simplicity's sake, I have used the masculine pronoun in preference to 'he/she' throughout. This in no way implies that no marketing managers are women.

Marketing Improvements Group Plc,   M.T. Wilson
Ulster House,   March 1988
Ulster Terrace,
Regent's Park,
London NW1

Acknowledgements

It is impossible to acknowledge individually the hundreds of people to whom I owe so much of this book. First, there are the directors, managers and staff of our clients, working with whom over the last twenty-five years provided the experiences on which this book is based.

Second, there are my colleagues in Marketing Improvements who have expanded and often improved my comprehension of the complex world of marketing. Again there are too many to mention by name, but I must single out the top management team – John Lidstone, David Senton, Peter Kirkby, Richard Martin, Patrick Forsyth and David Laing, with and through whom I have learnt so much.

M.T.W.

Part I

WHERE ARE WE NOW?

Chapter 1

Marketing in a Changing World

It is the prime task of the Marketing Director in conjunction with his top management colleagues to decide the corporate marketing objectives and strategies. However, it is impossible to plot the future direction of the organization realistically unless it is known where the company stands now in relation to its environment and its competitors. It might seem almost naive to suggest that a firm does not know its current position. However, in our experience because of the speed and complexity of change, all too often management fails to recognize its full implications or react sufficiently quickly or appropriately, preferring to believe either that change is not happening or, if it is, sooner or later 'things' will get back to 'normal'. The acceptance that change is happening and will continue to do so at an ever-increasing rate is the first step towards gaining a more accurate picture of the current position.

What was 'normal'?

To gain a true understanding of the nature, degree and implications of change, the top management team should reflect on what normality was and how far it still influences their attitudes today. Traditionally in most organizations, it was reasonable to believe in the almost unfettered and centralized power of management to achieve results through other people. The results to be achieved had to satisfy, in order of priority, the share-holders, the consumers and the staff.

The fundamental drive of the business was therefore towards growth of profits, usually from growth of volume. Sales increases would always be possible as markets grew. Increasing numbers of consumers could be persuaded to buy more through increased promotional expenditure;

3

distribution channels would support the manufacturer's efforts to sell more of his brands. The basic costs of the business – labour, materials and services – albeit increasing, did so within a predictable and relatively constant structure. There was little intervention from government and what there was could be regarded as temporary and peripheral irritation. There was, of course, competition to be contended with, but this came usually from other similar manufacturers run by similar managements.

Management practice in such an environment, not surprisingly, focused on profitability, long-term growth plans, concentration on the home market, selling home-produced products to traditional export markets, annual price changes, utilizing distribution networks as 'channels' through which products could be transmitted to the ever-persuadable consumer. Virtually every element of that normality has changed or been changed in less than twenty years, and even more rapidly than that for many companies. Most important of all, the two cornerstones of traditional management practice, certainty and centralized power, have been eroded, in some cases completely.

'Certainty' meant treating various elements as fixed or 'givens': that markets grow, that cost structures remain stable, that distribution channels distribute the brands the manufacturer chooses.

'Centralized power' meant that management had the absolute right and the means to decide what products would be made, how they would be marketed and at what price, how many people would be employed and where. The development of large computers processing, increasingly rapidly, vast quantities of data directly transmitted from all over the world if necessary, further enhanced this centralized power. No wonder the corporate head office felt it had the means to plan and control its global business in a predictable world.

Economic, political, social, legislative and technological forces have together destroyed that normality. Most if not all the basic assumptions on which management practices were predicated have to be reconsidered. The precepts of certainty and centralized power need urgent re-examination to identify what if anything is certain, and where the power now lies. Markets have changed and are changing in terms of needs, structure and location; distribution networks are evolving very rapidly in their nature and their patterns; costs are increasingly volatile because of inflation, currency fluctuation and economic and political changes. As more of the elements of the marketing system change faster, management must review them more often; yet many companies still put vast amounts of time and effort into detailed long-term planning which is inevitably and rapidly outdated.

Management power, in the traditional sense, is now flowing away from the manufacturer under the pressure of the environmental forces mentioned above. Consumers, distributors, suppliers, national and international government are all increasing their influence on the activities of the firm. Even within the organization, the power of central management is being eroded by social and technological change. Employee interests, represented by unions or not, increasingly have to be considered. The development of personal computing means that information power can and in many cases should now be decentralized to outlying subsidiaries, branches or departments if they are to be made fully effective and competitive.

Each individual organization will be, of course, affected differently by these forces of change; each management team must reach its own conclusions about what was 'normal' and what is today's actual and tomorrow's likely reality. The Marketing Director should be well-positioned to lead such reviews as he more than any of his colleagues carries the responsibility for controlling the interface between the company and its environment. Such assessments should start with examining economic, political, social, legislative and technological change, and how these have affected the markets, the distribution networks and the policies and practices of the company. (See Figure 1.1.) Against this backcloth, the main

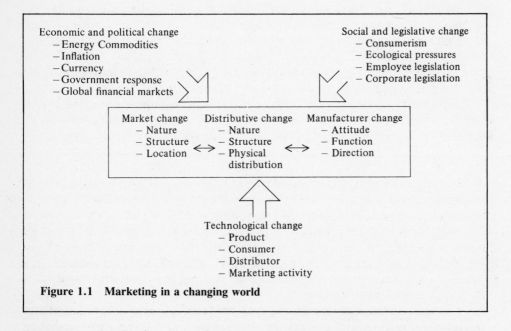

Figure 1.1 Marketing in a changing world

elements of the corporate marketing activity such as products, prices, distribution and promotion need to be evaluated to ensure that they are still satisfying consumer needs competitively and profitably. Such reviews of the changing environment and the corporate response to it should provide clear indicators of the company's strengths and weaknesses and the problems and opportunities facing it; and a knowledge of these is the base on which future objectives and strategies can be founded.

Economic and political change

The oil crisis sparked off by the Middle East war of Autumn 1973 is, of course, well recognized today as a fact of history. Society as a whole, and more particularly business management, were only too painfully aware of its effect on all forms of energy consumption – transportation, heating, lighting, power, etc., – as well as on the cost of oil-based products such as plastics. Its dramatic effect on the economies of the world was reviewed endlessly by the media. Perhaps, however, the deeper implications have not yet been recognized as fully as they need to be by management. What the oil crisis really signified was the end of the age of certainty, the upsetting of traditional structures and balances in the world and especially in the business environment. For the oil crisis demonstrated that any group possessing resources that were needed by others had much more power than traditionally had been recognized or wielded.

Realization of this new-found power slowly spread among many different commodity-producing nations, and led them to reappraise their role as suppliers to and consumers of Western manufacturers.

Country after country strove for the control and development of its own industry using whatever power it had in terms of resources, political control or economic influence to force investment in local enterprises to replace imports from abroad. For many countries, however, local investment in manufacturing can only be justified in terms of exporting at least part of the output, thus causing further change in international trade patterns.

Rising costs of energy and raw materials and changes in import/export balances fuelled inflation in different countries at different rates, but overall sufficiently to destroy international exchange rate stability.

Marketing in a changing world

The response of the commodity-consuming countries likewise has had a dramatic effect on the world economy. In general terms, such countries have not only tried to reduce or substitute their consumption of scarce expensive raw materials but also have attempted to increase their international trade to produce the export earnings to finance the commodity purchases they have to make.

This has caused a further swing of the economic pendulum as manufacturing countries such as Japan, Korea and Taiwan increased their exports into major economies such as the USA creating large-scale trade imbalances and the weakening of the US dollar. Simultaneously, commodity-rich nations like Malaysia, having geared its economy to high prices, now suffers with the reduction of price and demand for its raw materials such as tin, palm oil, timber, rubber and even oil itself, despite having established a broader manufacturing base, e.g. car production.

This ever-increasing international interplay of supply and demand has been further fuelled by the increasing globalization of financial markets which enables investment monies to be moved around the world at accelerating velocity; as was evidenced by the worldwide stock market crashes of October 1987 and the reverberating financial fluctuations that followed them.

The increasing volatility of international economies, the effect on growth rates, currency values, inflation etc., and the response from the various national and supranational governments from protectionism to monetarism, all mean that the Marketing Director and his colleagues must be much more knowledgeable about, and sensitive to, global as well as national issues. It may mean that some markets quickly become unattractive (e.g. Nigeria was one of the top overseas markets for British exporters only a few years ago but this market has now declined dramatically). It may mean that previously attractive prices have been destroyed by adverse currency movements as is currently the case for many European countries selling to the USA. Conversely, these two examples may well have been reversed by the time this is published. Few can predict the longer-term fluctuations of an increasing global and volatile economy. All managers need to recognize that global and volatile nature, to ensure that they are up to date and sensitive to it and to make rapid decisions to minimize the problems it causes and to maximize the exploitation of the opportunities afforded, e.g. the boost given to the European and Japanese holiday and travel industries as the US became a low-cost destination following the stock market crash and dollar depreciation.

Social and legislative forces

The change in social attitudes towards business and the legislative backing given to such changes is demanding increasing attention from management. It demonstrates again the changing balance of power between the manufacturer and his environment.

Throughout the '70s in Europe, and particularly in the USA, there was a growing groundswell of reaction against the apparent lack of concern by industry for anything other than financial success. The consumerist movement, led by people like Ralph Nader, showed that certain products not only did not perform as promised, but were in fact positively dangerous. His successful attack on the motor industry, forcing the recall of thousands of unsafe cars, was but the start of an ever-widening circle of concern about the real effects of products on the consumer and later their effect on the environment. Tragedies such as the thalidomide disaster, growing worries about pollution of the landscape, the waterways, the atmosphere and even the stratosphere in the case of aerosol propellants, have all combined to create a heightened sensitivity among individual consumers, consumer and ecologically concerned groups, and eventually government. Industries as diverse as cars, pharmaceuticals, packaging, toiletries and food have all had to face extra legislation at both national and international levels, specifying not only how their products should be developed and manufactured, but also how they can be marketed in terms of product specification, pricing, promotion, distribution and competition.

Regardless of the particular political complexion of the government of the day, it is hard to see how this tide of opinion will ever turn. There seems little doubt that companies will have to heed these social attitudes, particularly as they are being continuously reinforced by more education, publicity and supranational legislation from bodies such as the EC.

This redressing of the balance of power between the consumer and the supplier, between the goals of the commercial organization and the needs of the environment and society, is mirrored in the changing relationship between the employee and the employer. The rights of the employee in terms of dismissal, sickness, redundancy, even pregnancy, have been enshrined in a mass of legislation; again it should be noted by those who saw this process as the machinations of a particular government, that even now, the employee in Britain is still not as well protected as in most countries in Western Europe. As Britain further harmonizes her laws and regulations with the EC, more rather than less such legislation can be expected.

Top management reading this section will of course have their own opinions on whether these social trends and the legislation in which they are embodied are desirable or not, depending on their own political persuasions. It is not the task of this book to argue for or against them but to identify their existence and their impact on the marketing activities of the firm. There seems little doubt that the attitudes described above are neither caused by a specific political party nor restricted to a specific country. There is a general social and legislative movement, particularly in what is termed the developed world, towards protection of the environment, the consumer and the employee, controlling product specification, pricing, distribution and promotion, and encouraging greater competition between organizations to further improve their offerings to their markets. It is unrealistic to believe that the 'good old days' of hiring and firing, fixing price increases with competition, limiting distributors' business activities, etc., will ever return. It may be wiser to reflect that marketing activity is always surrounded by constraints, whether these be problems of demand, lack of distribution outlets, shortage of supply or inability to find enough good salesmen, etc. Today we face a different set of parameters and it is the essence of the management tack to achieve results in this altered environment. There is much evidence that those companies which take positive initiatives towards these social changes can gain considerably in commercial terms. Marks and Spencer, for example, has a justifiably high reputation among consumers for value for money, safety consciousness, immediate refunds if the buyer changes his or her mind, and other consumer-oriented services, and at the same time achieves considerable profitability and growth.

Technological change

The Marketing Director, though not necessarily an expert himself, must be aware of the impact on the environment and his firm in particular, of dramatic technological changes, notably in electronics. The development of the microprocessor and its large-scale production has revolutionized information collection, processing and dissemination which in turn is affecting the whole spectrum of marketing activity.

The impact on product technology has obviously been significant, for example, making computing available to every schoolchild. There are, however, many wider and less well-publicized implications that should be as much the concern of top marketing management as any direct product applications.

First, the development of cheaper, smaller computers means that the customer, whether a retailer or an end-user of industrial products such as an engineering plant, can now collect and process information on, for example, rates of sale or usage, stock movements or profit margins, so accurately and quickly that the whole cycle of consumption, changes in sale or usage, stock levels, and therefore recording can become virtually automatic. For example, there are already retail stores where the products are marked with a light-sensitive bar code representing the unique article number which can be 'read' by the check-out cash register which then not only prints out the bill for the customer, but also the stock position of the item and the recording that is needed to replace the stock to a predetermined level. By linking the store's computer to that of the suppliers, the order can be automatically placed, thus eliminating an accpeted function of most sales forces. A similar system can be installed where an industrial customer is purchasing consumables, for instance bearings, from a manufacturer.

Furthermore, if the retailer wishes to allocate his shelf space optimally it is possible to use the computer to do this traditional job of the merchandiser. For example, we developed a computer programme with a toy company which, given the sizes, rates of demand and profit margins of the various toys in the range, will allocate them to fill, at optimum profit, the retailer's available shelf space.

The roles of the salesman and merchandiser are likely to be changed by such developments; the salesman's function will be further modified by the use of the remote entry hand-held microterminal. This resembles a pocket calculator which can be coupled via a normal telephone to the firm's main computer. The salesman, while negotiating with the buyer, can check, for example, current product availability immediately with the main computer and when the sale is completed, enter the order directly. The computer can thus print out dispatch notes and invoices without having to wait for the salesman's order to arrive in the post in the usual way. In one food company where the procedure has been installed, the cost of the whole system was recouped within 12 months from the cash flow savings resulting from the more rapid order processing, compared with the two- or three-day delay inherent in the previous manual and postal routines of the salesman. A further refinement is that it is possible to link the computer to a closed circuit TV system so that when the Area Manager arrives home in the evening he can study on his domestic TV receiver, a report of the sales results of his salesmen that day.

The same type of domestic closed circuit TV system can be used to give shopping information to the housewife such as which store has special offers, etc. This has considerable implications for the traditional advertising and promotional activities of the firm.

Market research analysis, sales forecasting, sales planning and control systems are other areas of marketing activity which are being fundamentally affected by these cheaper, more powerful electronic methods of data collection, processing and communication. Perhaps the most significant impact of cheaper, more powerful, information technology is in the area of database management. It is now possible to collect information about present and potential customers, store it, manipulate and access it, in ways that were not feasible five years ago.

This means that many organizations no longer have to regard their markets *en masse*; they can target their communications very precisely, thus dramatically increasing their cost-effectiveness. This has revolutionized, even created, the whole area of direct marketing – mail shots, telephone selling, targeted mailing, leaflet drops, newsletters etc. For example, a bank with literally millions of customers traditionally had to promote new services such as home improvement loans on a blanket basis, relying on a response from those to whom the product applied. Today, given the effort to build the database, the same bank could target accurately only those customers who owned homes and, if desired, more specific categories such as first-time buyers.

There is little doubt that technology can now help provide many answers, but only if management asks the right questions! It is therefore important that the Marketing Director reviews the whole spectrum of his marketing activity to ensure that no opportunities are being missed to put these kinds of development to work. One of the reasons why the possibilities are often insufficiently examined is that many management teams feel threatened and fear that these electronic devices will eliminate the need for them and their staff. However, an objective analysis will show quickly that the work being taken over by the new technology is mainly the routine paperwork and processes of the company. Electronic ordering should free the salesman from routine order taking and allow much more time for the creative sales process.

Computerized shelf allocation leaves the merchandiser free to develop new display concepts, introduce new products, create novel promotions and furthermore, enables simulation of their likely effects. Given that the computer can process management information faster and display it better, the executive team can concentrate their attention on improving their decision making, rather than ploughing through lengthy reports looking for significant data.

The electronic revolution offers impressive opportunities for those marketing teams that are positive and objective enough to identify and exploit them. Those firms that choose, for whatever reason, to ignore the possibilities, are likely to find themselves at a serious cost and profit disadvantage, particularly as personnel costs rise.

Conclusion

It is a well-accepted paradox that the only constant is change, but the speed, the acceleration and the growing complexity of change can confuse even the most aware Marketing Director; worse still it can cause top management either to pretend it is not happening or react entirely negatively in the vain attempt to prevent it happening. The most difficult and dangerous situation, however, is when there is an apparent recognition but it is at such a superficial level that there is no fundamental change in management attitudes and practices.

This chapter has not attempted to predict the future; that task is left to clairvoyants and futurologists. What it says is that there are great strands of economic, political, social, legislative and technological change weaving their way through the whole fabric of society, which will continue to transform, often dramatically, the environment in which top marketing management must operate. Because of the difficulties of forecasting the future accurately, the best approach is often to monitor the present even more widely and regularly in order to identify, at the earliest possible moment, changes which demand action.

Some features of the future landscape are however beginning to be better delineated.

First, more and more markets are becoming globalized where the same (or very similar) heavily branded product or service is produced and marketed internationally. This is already happening in markets such as soft drinks, cars, cigarettes, fast food, car rental and home electronics. As a consequence international competitive pressures are increasing. Any national manufacturer or service supplier must look beyond his home boundaries if he is not to be taken unawares by such multinational competitors. For example, many national TV and hi-fi suppliers in Europe were driven out of business by the global marketing strength of the Japanese manufacturers.

Second, to respond to these increasing global competitive pressures demands a change in the way in which companies conceive their marketing philosophy. It is no longer sufficient to view marketing simply as the process that identifies and satisfies consumers at a profit as if each firm functioned in a vacuum insulated from competition. Today, the true nature of marketing is perhaps better defined as 'the strategic and profitable creation and maintenance of need-satisfying differences *v.* competition'.

Viewing the marketing process in this way places a different and more practical emphasis on marketing activity. It highlights the need for national and multinational competitor surveillance and analysis. It forces the company to decide how it will differentiate itself from its competitors in ways that will enable it to better satisfy the market: by offering more desirable products or services, more convenient ways of purchasing or using them, better after-sales service, or better prices or credit terms etc. Finally, it specifies that the differentiation process must be conceived at a strategic level meaning globally as well as throughout the whole organization.

Third, it has often been said that marketing is too important to be left to the marketing department. Today, it is clear that marketing concepts and processes must pervade the total enterprise. Successful companies create a marketing culture where everyone in the firm recognizes that they must make a contribution to satisfying customers better than competitors.

To achieve this means ensuring that the basics of marketing are in place and working effectively; that products are designed to satisfy customer needs not R & D's technical interests; that products are manufactured to the standard and performance promised and that production staff understand what that means; that customer enquiries, orders, service demands and complaints are dealt with promptly and efficiently and that all personnel involved with customer contact are selected, trained and motivated to do so.

Even though the world is changing in an ever-increasingly volatile way with markets and competitors becoming more global as shown by the numerous studies referred to earlier, those organizations who ensure that these fundamental marketing principles are implemented rigorously and continuously will continue to make consistent profitable progress.

The continuing success of such different businesses as IBM and McDonalds and the resurgence of corporations like Jaguar and British Airways results more than anything else from doing the simple things well. They all in their different ways ensure that their products or services are designed to satisfy consumer needs, that their offerings live up to the expectations promised and that their customers are cared for before, during and after purchase and usage. Perhaps most important of all, they differentiate themselves from their competitors by being a little better at all these key points thus persuading customers to prefer them.

CHECKLIST

1 *Economic and political change*

1.1 How is our cost structure being affected by national and international fluctuations?
1.2 How are our markets being affected?
1.3 Is our pricing policy coping with inflation and currency rate instability?
1.4 Do we recognize the full implications of economic and political change on all the traditional bases of corporate policy?

2 *Social and legislative forces*

2.1 How are we reacting to consumerism?
2.2 How are we affected by national and international legislation on products, prices, distribution and promotion?
2.3 Are we aware of the implications of employee legislation at home and abroad?

3 *Technological change*

3.1 What is the effect of technological change, especially in electronics, on our products or services?
3.2 What is the effect on the consumers?
3.3 What is the effect on distributor activities?
3.4 What is the effect on our sales and marketing activities?

4 *Our organization*

4.1 Do we accept the impact of economic/political, social/legislative and technology changes and their implications (e.g. globalization) on our business?
4.2 Have we redefined our marketing philosophy in terms of strategic competitive differences?
4.3 Have we created a customer value driven culture throughout the enterprise?
4.4 Overall, are we capable of doing the 'simple' marketing things better than the competition to the increasing satisfaction of our consumers?

Chapter 2

Market and Distributive Change

Most managements try to keep up-to-date with the complex and changing marketplace by commissioning research, visiting customers and distribution outlets, discussing with their sales forces, and even talking to the competition! This can give the appearance of detailed knowledge of the markets on which operating decisions can be taken; the reality is sadly often very different. In practice there is sometimes so much research data that management cannot find time to analyse and digest it in depth. When research findings conflict with the conventional wisdom in the company, the validity of the research is often questioned, rather than the subjective opinions of the marketing/sales team.

In one company where research showed that the European market was about to stagnate after a period of considerable growth, the Market Research Manager himself came under heavy suspicion from top management for having negative attitudes! Fortunately for him, events proved him right: sadly for the company, insufficient action had been taken quickly enough to prepare for the market downturn.

Furthermore, unless sales force, trade, customer and competitor opinions are collected and analysed very carefully, they can be misleading. Many marketing staff seem to confuse knowing the market well with what in practice is often the case: knowing that part of the market they happen to be servicing at the moment. It is often forgotten too that sales force views are usually based on their buyers' interpretations of what they think is happening in the marketplace and then sometimes further biased by the negotiating relationship between them.

The changing marketplace

Given such realities, the Marketing Director needs to reassess from time to

14

time the basic assumptions and data about the market to ensure that he and his colleagues have a sound basis for planning. This can involve regular reconsideration of some fundamental questions to ensure the company is still perceiving the marketplace accurately.

First, do the consumer needs that have been satisfied in the past continue to exist and be satisfied by the same products or services? The need for personal timekeeping continues to exist, but the Swiss watch industry was slow to believe that it could be better satisfied by electronic digital timepieces. This identification of consumer or end-user need, fundamental and critical though it self-evidently is, can be very difficult to achieve in many industrial markets where a basic product, like steel, is used for many different final applications. However, although it may be difficult to identify and quantify each different market segment, it is important that the company has a clear concept of at least the major categories of need to be satisfied, and how those needs and competitive satisfactions are evolving. As a simple instance, aluminium was considered traditionally too expensive a material for large-scale use in automobile manufacture. The need to reduce fuel consumption by reducing the weight of the car is now making aluminium a feasible alternative to steel, for years the only choice. In the consumer market, a study by Nielsen* of the reasons why brand leaders lost their pre-eminence showed that 67 per cent had slipped because of failure to keep the product up to date, i.e. in line with consumer needs and competitive satisfactions.

One significant factor that needs to be monitored in many markets is the source of competitive satisfactions – other domestic manufacturers, imports or retailer owned brands – as this may indicate that different marketing strategies are needed.

Second, is the marketplace changing in nature? Most companies recognize changes in the scale of the market: increasing, decreasing or static. Less well perceived may be the changes in the nature of the market such as swings from one segment to another. The construction industry, for example, declined dramatically during the latter half of the '70s and every supplier recognized the fact. Far less obvious was a switch from new construction to refurbishment of older property which offered considerable opportunity for builders and materials and components suppliers, though this was not quickly identified by many such companies. Not only was their market information insufficiently detailed and therefore unable to identify the movements in the various segments, but also their traditional marketing methods via architects and large developers and contractors did not reach the company secretaries, maintenance managers and local builders who specify and purchase in the refurbishment sector.

With such examples in mind, the Marketing Director should check the current validity of the company's market segmentation criteria. All the well-accepted bases of market segmentation – geographic, demographic, consumer need, customer size, distribution channel, etc. – are dynamic and change relatively, as well as in absolute terms.

**Why advertise established brands?* Nielsen Researcher no. 3, 1976.

The alcoholic drinks industry demonstrates the case well. Over the last few years there have been major changes in consumer tastes, (e.g. a swing towards lighter beers, the resurgence of 'real ale', the growth in wine consumption). Also segmentation based on demographic characteristics has had to be reconsidered. Foreign holidays, increased eating out, changes in levels of disposable income, have all contributed to the confusion of traditional relationships between socio-economic characteristics and drink preferences. Furthermore, there has been a marked swing towards the take-home trade and away from on-licence consumption. This has been caused and affected by social and distributive change – the development of specialist drink outlets, the licensing of supermarkets and other non-traditional stores. In turn, this has led to the development of new major independent customers. Even some of the classic geographic segmentation of home and export markets, separated at least in pricing strategy, has been destroyed by the EEC Commission forcing the Scotch whisky producers to sell the same brands on the same pricing structure throughout member countries.

All these changes in the nature of the market have had to be reflected in the products, prices and promotion activities of the breweries, distilleries and vineyards serving it. Own label brands, new packaging concepts (e.g. plastic wine bottles), price cutting, more creative and expensive promotion are some examples of the attempts to react to the dynamic marketplace.

Third, is the marketplace changing in strucure? The buying power in most markets is not evenly spread; big customers tend to grow bigger, small customers are becoming more difficult and expensive to service.

A regular check on the market structure is necessary to see how far and how fast such trends are progressing because of the impact on the marketing activity of the firms. As has been seen in so many industries, from food to motor components, big customers can demand different products (often under their own name), keener prices and terms and specific promotional sales and servicing activities. Furthermore, the big customers now co-ordinate buying internationally which places even greater demands upon their suppliers.

A salutary exercise for most companies is to list the ten top buyers in the market five years ago and the percentage of the total market they then occupied and compare this with today's statistics. Most firms will see a dramatically increased polarization, which is usually magnified even further if the exercise is repeated in terms of the company's own major customers and the percentage of total company sales they represent today compared with the past.

Fourth, is the marketplace changing in location? The '70s and '80s saw a fundamental rearrangement of international economics. However, there are many companies which continue to operate on traditional home and export concepts, more suited to trading in a bygone age. Today, the continental European markets should be the natural prime opportunities for most British manufacturers. Yet still we find too many firms who know little and do less about them. Further afield, the perspective of the firm is often limited to Commonwealth territories or the apparently wealthy oil-rich nations which can cause major opportunities to be overlooked in areas such as Latin America or Asia.

The change in the international marketplace is mirrored by the change in the pattern of international supply. Competition has become more international and, depending on the industry, may well be so powerful that it will be difficult for European manufacturers to survive unless they change their marketing stance fundamentally. One UK footwear company, for example, concluded that it could not compete with the labour and raw material cost advantages of Far Eastern manufacturers. It has therefore become largely a merchanting company buying from its previous competitors and putting its resources behind maintenance of its own brand name and position by more powerful marketing activity than it could previously afford. A European industrial component manufacturer, recognizing that none of its national subsidiaries could compete individually on price against Japanese suppliers, reduced its production costs by concentrating each country on manufacturing only part of the product range for the whole group, thus achieving significant economies of scale. However, this action demanded major reorganization of the marketing and distribution activities as each national organization had to change from the simpler situation of producing and selling for its own home market.

Changes in distribution patterns

For many companies the only economic way to reach consumers or end-users is through some form of distributive network. All too often, however, there seems to be an assumption that traditional channels will continue to exist as in the past, and will be basically responsive to the requirements of the manufacturer. This attitude of regarding distribution networks as 'constants' can be demonstrated from many marketing plans which treat products, prices and promotion as 'variables', predict changes in population patterns, consumer buying habits or technology, but seldom forecast in the same detail changes in the distribution system.

In reality, however, distribution patterns seem to be changing with increasing rapidity as they respond to movements in consumer demand and purchasing habits on the one hand, and developing product technology on the other. It is possible, given a long enough time scale, to identify an evolutionary process in distribution systems. Table 2.1 lists some of the main characteristics of each stage of this process.

Distribution systems are always evolving; the problem is managements' perception of this evolution against a traditional view of them as constant or reactive. For example, in a study for a consumer durable company, we showed that 20 per cent of the market was being supplied by a network that had not existed five years previously and in which the company had no representation.

In another case, an industrial component supplier who had concentrated traditionally on original equipment (OE) business, was faced with stagnation in that market segment. Turning his attention to the replacement

Table 2.1
Major phases of evolution of distribution systems

Phase 1	Large numbers of small independent outlets stocking a limited product range within well-defined trades. E.g. in 1971 84.2% of confectionery and tobacconist trade handled by independent traders.
Phase 2	Emergence of retailing groups expanding geographically by purchase or opening outlets. Larger multiples begin to buy direct, thus putting pressure on wholesalers who may respond by forming groups with small retailers. E.g. Burtons purchasing Jackson the tailors with concentration in Tyneside and Scotland. Emergence of voluntary group movement (VG, Mace, Spar, etc.)
Phase 3	Large retail groups expanding by addition of product ranges in ever larger stores. E.g. Boots the chemists diversifying into photographic equipment, books, toys, babywear, etc. Tesco into home and clothing products.
Phase 4	Large retail groups developing own business concept and moving away from being purely a channel for suppliers' brands. Development of private label evolving towards retailer brands. E.g. Marks & Spencer 'St Michael' brand sold to other retailers in over 50 countries.
Phase 5	Large groups competing fiercely with each other for market share (e.g. by price cutting) as market flattens and geographic and product expansion possibilities diminish. E.g. Tesco/Sainsbury price war in late '70s/early '80s.
Phase 6	Number of large groups declines because of acquisition or simply ceasing trading. Those that are left in an increasingly dominant position and strong enough to diversify into other trades. The small shops only survive by specialization and/or personalized service. E.g. W. H. Smith into DIY.

market, he found that he knew virtually nothing about how it worked. Although he had been selling to distributors, he had little idea about to whom they sold, how they sold, the changing patterns of networks, etc. He was thus in a very weak position to select or influence them at a time when they were fast becoming his most important customers in revenue and profit terms.

Distribution networks change not only in nature and importance, but also in structure. Mature networks are typified, not by large numbers of small weak outlets, but by relatively few, very large and powerful distributors who control the whole industry nationally and who are now expanding internationally. This evolution can be clearly seen in the grocery and chemist trades; whether manufacturers saw it early enough or are even now reacting strongly enough must still be questioned. With hindsight, it does appear that because of the lack or inappropriateness of the manufacturers' response to this polarization of their networks, they have in many cases helped to cause a situation which today is very much against them. The balance of power in the food industry, for example, has swung in favour of the retailer as opposed to the manufacturers, as can be seen from the relative profitability of the two. In 1985/86, food distributors showed an average return on capital employed of 23.0 per cent while food manufacturers only achieved 17.3 per cent.*

The conditions affecting physical distribution activities (stock holding,

Industrial Performance Analysis, 12th edition, Business Ratios Division of Inter Company Comparisons Ltd, 1987.

warehousing, transport) are also changing. Rapidly rising energy prices and property, equipment and labour costs have caused distribution to become the largest single expense for many companies. Obviously changes in market structures, distributive patterns and road networks have also modified the preconditions on which many warehouse sizes and locations were originally based. The evolution of materials handling technology too has had an effect which is often not appreciated. For example, in two cases in which we were involved, the pricing and discount structures of the companies concerned had not reflected changes in materials handling and transport. The result in one case was that any customer placing an order at the best quantity discount required one and a half delivery trucks or two-thirds of a trunking vehicle to deliver it. In the other case there was no relationship between the quantity discounts and pallet sizes, although both the manufacturer and his customers were entirely palletized and preferred to deal in pallet loads only.

If a review of distribution is important in the UK market, it is vital overseas; in most export markets, distribution is the fundamental factor for future success. Millions of words have been spent (wasted?) on Britain's delivery record overseas, but the problem is usually much deeper than the simple exhortations to do better might suggest. The evaluation and selection of overseas distributive networks should be regarded as a critical senior management responsibility embracing a thorough knowledge of the market to be served, the networks and distributive methods available (often totally different from those in the UK) and the legal and financial implications. This at least might help to avoid the difficult situation in which one major British manufacturer found himself in the USA. Having granted exclusive rights to a distributor who subsequently also took on a competitive product range, he discovered too late that by the laws of the state concerned he could not change the distributor without heavy compensation. His assumption that exclusivity worked both ways was sadly totally unfounded, and he was thus tied exclusively to a distributor selling competitive products. In most countries it is prudent to assume that the law will favour the local distributor rather than the 'foreign' importer; thus any contractual arrangements need to be made with great care and attention and the best local legal advice money can buy.

The importance of reviewing the distribution system cannot be doubted. In many firms distribution networks must be used to get products to market, distribution costs occupy an increasing percentage of total cost structure, overseas distribution arrangements are critical to export success all at a time when the nature and the structure of the total distribution activity is changing rapidly. Yet the examples quoted (and they are not isolated ones) suggest fundamental errors, both of omission and commission, in management decision making. We believe that this is because there is seldom a total distribution concept within the firm with the result that there is insufficient consideration of distribution implications upon corporate policy and strategy. This, and the scattering of distribution responsibilties across various management functions, mean that decision making tends to be departmental and short-term.

Thus, in the case of the component manufacturer, as long as the OE markets were buoyant, it was nobody's job to analyse replacement market distribution, although it was inevitable and predictable that the replacement market would become relatively much more important. In the case of the consumer durable company, the sales department sold to existing outlets; it had no brief to search for new outlets because nobody had imagined that a new network would develop and it had good representation in the traditional ones. In the grocery trade, the short-term advantages of having fewer, larger customers blinded many manufacturers to the longer-term implications, particularly those who grabbed the immediate profit advantages of supplying own-label products. The temptation of long production runs and low marketing costs, albeit at lower prices compared with the tough and costly job of building a brand franchise, clouded the longer-term implications of loss of control of their own business, which many grocery manufacturers now regret. In 1979, sales of own brands accounted for 23 per cent (per cent by value) of packaged grocery sales. Own label has slowly increased its market share to 28 per cent of sales in 1985. For example, own brand bread now commands a 50 per cent share of standard bread sold in supermarkets.*

It is interesting to note that in markets which have not as yet reached the stage of evolution of the USA or Western Europe, the same mistakes are being made. In Australia, for example, one of the leading frozen food brands is already a retailer own-label. In discussing this with frozen food manufacturers there they could not perceive any long-term dangers. They saw only the advantages of not having to spend money on consumer production and the benefits of long production runs, and were by their actions causing the retailer own-label to become even more powerful.

The question of the state of evolution of overseas markets is of great significance to international marketing policy; unless manufacturers have a clear concept of what stage overseas distribution networks have reached, they will find it difficult to take the appropriate strategic and tactical decisions to influence them. This was exemplified by one international food company which had run, with spectacular failure, an up-to-date training programme for distributor salesmen in Morocco. They asked us to go back in our files to find the training programmes we ran in Western Europe ten years ago and they proved appropriate.

The examples of lack of congruence between pricing and discount structures and truck and pallet sizes typifies the common absence of a total distribution concept and integrated responsibility. The pricing decisions and the materials handling decisions separately may be perfectly valid; together they become a nonsense rather like the packaging design decision taken in a jam company which resulted in a much more modern and aesthetically appealing cap for the jar. It was only seen to be disastrous when retailers complained that their stacks of jars were falling over and thus refused to buy or display the product. The original design had had a rim which made for stable stacking, but those concerned with packaging design had no responsibility for and little knowledge of distribution.

*Key Note Report, 'Own Brand', 1986.

The complexity of overseas distribution usually demands a range of skills far beyond that provided by the typical export department, often, as the examples showed, in the legal area. It is unlikely that this expertise will be available within even large companies' Head Office legal departments as each country has such different legal requirements, particularly relating to importation and distribution. Mistakes can be expensive; it cost one large German manufacturer over £8 million in loss of profits compensation when he replaced his French distributor. A further international legal dimension is embodied in Article 85 of the EEC Treaty which prohibits exclusive distributive agreements except where it can be shown that these will benefit the consumer in terms of safety, efficiency, after-sales service etc.

The evaluation of distribution networks and activities has been dealt with here at length because it is a vital component of the marketing activity of so many companies and yet seems to be given insufficient top management attention, perhaps because there is seldom any one executive at senior level responsible for overseeing the whole distribution activity (i.e. policy, strategy, outlet management, physical distribution). This concept of looking at all the elements of the distribution function as an entity is useful in evaluating the corporate performance of that most basic task of commercial enterprise – the profitable movement of the products to the consumer.

Constructing 'market system maps'

The assessment of the impact of economic, political, social, legislative and technological forces on the market and the distribution networks that serve it can be highly complex. It can be difficult to envisage clearly the practical implications of such a review and thus decide the appropriate action. One approach that we have found valuable is to plot 'market system maps' which can show all the elements in the mechanism that exists between manufacturer and consumer in order to supply value satisfactions to the latter at a profit to the former.

Such maps should not only describe the various stages and flows in the system, but should also quantify, where possible, the relationships. The primary objective of such mapping is to give management a clearer view of how the mechanism works and thus to determine the appropriate influences to bring to bear on it. Unless the manufacturer perceives that, for example, today's consumer purchasing behaviour has changed, it is difficult to promote the relevant benefits or to distribute effectively.

The first stage in constructing such maps is to identify all the elements in the system. These include the major categories of consumers or end-users, distributors and customers, each of which may require subdivision (e.g. distributors into wholesalers and retailers). In addition the main influences on each element should be listed (e.g. professional specifiers, such as architects or doctors, or commercial specifiers, such as the maintenance engineer who briefs his buyer on the lubricants required). Where appropriate the influence of consumerists and ecological groups or of government should be noted.

Mapping should always start with the consumers or end-users, listing their characteristics:

1 Who they are (e.g. age, sex, occupation, socio-economic group etc.).
2 Their needs (e.g. convenience, taste, reliability, performance, cost, etc.).
3 How those needs are satisfied by direct competition (i.e. similar products to ours) and indirect competition (different products or services which satisfy the same need).
4 Where the consumer obtains the product (e.g. supermarket, industrial dealer or direct from manufacturer).

A study of such characteristics can also lead to a reconsideration of the company's market segmentation criteria.

Even at this early stage of mapping, we often find that there is insufficient data available, but at least this helps define future research requirements.

Working back from the consumer, the next stage is to identify the outlets from which they purchase and the features of those outlets, considering:

1 What are their needs (e.g. products which will sell easily, prices which allow attractive profit margins, continuity of supply, ease of display, etc.)?
2 How are those needs now satisfied (i.e. what do we and competition do to satisfy them)?

Depending on the product, there may be other stages which must be analysed in a similar way (see the glass container example shown in Figure 2.1).

Traditionally the manufacturer's view of the market in industries like packaging was based largely on information about his customers. Thus the glass container manufacturer's perspective and indeed marketing activity

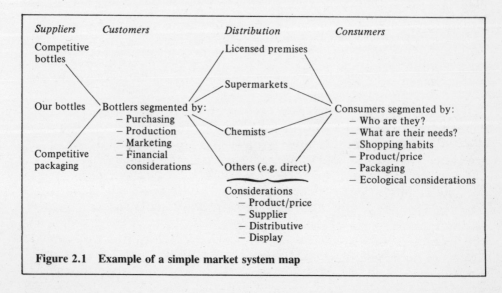

Figure 2.1   Example of a simple market system map

was largely determined by the bottlers who bought from him. The main promotional technique used was the sales force calling on the buyers of the bottlers. Not surprisingly, the purchasing criteria such as price, discounts and delivery were seen to be the chief needs to be satisfied. The market map shows, however, that there are other significant considerations such as production demands (e.g. bottling line standards, breakage rates, handling characteristics), financial needs (e.g. stock financing), and, particularly, marketing requirements (e.g. range of sizes, volumes, display, in-store and in-use characteristics). The bottler's marketing needs mostly reflect the demands of their customers and the distribution networks through which they sell, as well as their own product requirements. Thus a bottler selling soft drinks through both licensed premises and supermarkets may well have to use different types of container, even though the product is common. In turn, the needs of the distributive channels in terms of sizes, display characteristics, distributive arrangements, etc. are directly influenced by the consumers they serve as well as their own business requirements. Thus the attractiveness of the bottle on the shelf to the housewife must be of prime concern to the supermarket buyer, whereas it is much less important in the public house where the drinker is served by the barstaff.

To construct market maps like this involves the compilation of large amounts of data from the internal records and experience of the company, and usually external research at each level. It may seem impractical, particularly for industrial manufacturers, to conduct consumer and distributor research as well as collect information about their own customers.

However, a simple analysis such as that of the glass container market should clearly demonstrate the marketing truth that only by understanding how demand is derived ultimately from the final consumer can the manufacturer plot his own future direction. It was such research that led to the original development of the one-trip bottle by a glass manufacturer who identified the need for such a container by recognizing the trend in consumer purchasing of soft drinks away from the traditional off-licence outlets which had established bottle return systems and to the supermarkets which did not. This in turn caused ecological issues to be raised which must now be regarded as an important influence in any packaging market system.

Research is needed to establish not only market sizes, segments, shares, distribution channel volumes etc., but also the changing patterns of needs, attitudes and opinions at all levels in the market map. Many companies are now well served with quantitative research producing such statistics. Qualitative research, however, is far less well developed, although demonstrably as important For example, the attitudes of distributors to their suppliers can seriously affect the manufacturer's ability to market through them. One of our industrial clients mounted a sales expansion programme which although financially attractive to the distributors was not implemented with any enthusiasm. Subsequent research showed that the key reason was that the distributors feared that if they built up sales in their areas, the manufacturer might replace them with his own branch offices. This had happened in one or two cases some years previously where the distributors had proved inadequate for quite different reasons. On the basis of these findings, the campaign was reconstructed with adequate safeguards to allay the distributor's concerns.

A thorough understanding of the mechanisms of each market in which the company operates is essential if the future direction is to be plotted successfully; furthermore, by preparing market maps on a regular basis, trends can be identified more easily and future change more accurately predicted.

An example of a more complex map is shown in Figure 2.2. This

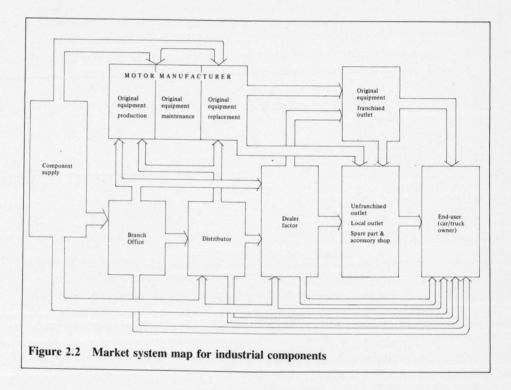

Figure 2.2   Market system map for industrial components

illustrates the routes by which a particular industrial component was supplied to the major segments of the motor manufacturer for both production line and maintenance use, and to the car or truck owner for replacement purposes. By quantifying the volumes travelling along each route, and the price at which each transaction was made, it was possible for our client to choose which of the many possible ways of accessing the market was likely to be most effective. Without such a map it was difficult to appreciate the complexity of the mechanism involved and thus to select the best approach.

CHECKLIST

1 *The changing marketplace*

1.1 How are the consumer needs in which we are interested changing, especially in the ways in which they are satisfied?
1.2 Is the total market changing in nature?
1.3 Is it changing in structure?
1.4 Is it changing in location?

2 *Changes in distribution patterns*

2.1 How are the networks changing in nature?
2.2 How are they changing in structure?
2.3 Have the factors affecting physical distribution changed?
2.4 How are international distribution patterns evolving?

3 *Competitive analysis*

3.1 How are our direct competitors changing?
3.2 How are our indirect competitors changing?
3.3 Who are our potential competitors?
3.4 Could our customers become our competitors?

4 *Constructing 'market system maps'*

4.1 Can we specify accurately our consumers' characteristics today?
4.2 Have we reviewed our market segmentation criteria recently?
4.3 Have we an up-to-date understanding of the needs of our distributors and/or customers?
4.4 Have we a clear picture of the activities of direct and indirect competition?
4.5 Do we have sufficient qualitative as well as quantitative research data?

Note
The questions are all posed in the present within the context of more accurately identifying 'where we are now'. Each question should also be considered in the future tense in order to try to predict the environment within which the firm will have to operate.

Chapter 3

The Marketing Audit – 1

Assessing the changing environment in which the company operates can be complex enough, but at least it can usually be done with some objectivity. The evaluation of the current performance of the firm within the environment is a more difficult task because it implies judging the results of previous management action. Because of the natural human tendency to rationalize, it is important that today's position is assessed systematically, with great care and objectivity.

The concept of the marketing audit is based on the financial audit in that it is a regular external review of the activities of the organization. The financial audit is of course intended to check the accuracy of the internal accounting system, suggest any improvements in it and verify the financial results for the shareholders. The marketing audit is designed to assess the competitive effectiveness of the marketing activities of the company, identify strengths and weaknesses in the operation and report the findings to top management. This should furnish an objective basis for future planning. In an increasingly complex, international and changing world, it is difficult for senior management to know how effective the marketing organization is without some form of regular monitoring. Results alone will only identify what has happened, not why it has happened, and as present results are caused by previous action (or lack of it), it may be too late to correct the situation.

The marketing audit looks at the competitive effectiveness of the current activities as well as at results, thus establishing a basis for predicting the likely outcome. Where audits are conducted regularly, comparison between findings provides an indication of trends.

The primary objective of the marketing activity is to supply value satisfactions at a profit to the company. The natural starting point for a marketing audit aimed at assessing how well that goal is being achieved is to check what satisfactions seem to be needed by the various levels of the marketing system – consumers, distributors and customers – and how well they are being provided by the company relative to competition. Such perception surveys can give a relative performance rating not only of the basic product/price offering, but also of the competitive effectiveness of the distribution methods and the promotional mix, thus providing the basic criteria for the more detailed review of each component of the marketing activity.

The contribution of the marketing activity to the commercial objectives of the firm must then be assessed using yardsticks derived from both the corporate targets and budgets, and where possible, other comparable organizations.

Using the external standards of the marketplace and the internal criteria of the firm as a basis, the key elements of the marketing activity should then be evaluated. Normally this will mean a detailed review of products (current performance, range, development process), pricing (approaches, structures, strategies), distribution activities (network selection, outlet management, physical distribution) and the promotional mix (PR, advertising, sales promotion and personal selling).

Marketing audits are usually best conducted by personnel outside the marketing management structure. It is difficult for line management to be totally objective about current performance and activities as they are so closely involved in them. Furthermore, a thorough audit can take more time than is normally available over and above everyday commitments. Some companies, therefore, use staff from other operating divisions or central management services; others use external consultants who not only have the time and the objectivity, but also should possess a broader expertise based on best current practice in other analogous companies or industries which can bring a further dimension to the evaluation process.

The perception survey

This approach aims to identify the current needs of the various groups of people that the company is trying to satisfy and evaluate how well those requirements are being met by the various competitive offerings.

The first stage, therefore, is to define the various groups of people through which the company markets its products or services from the 'market system map'. They will normally include purchasers, consumers or end-users in the various market segments selected by the firm, distributors (i.e. who purchase for resale) representing the different networks used, and, where applicable, customers (e.g. companies who purchase the product to incorporate it into their own product) or specifiers (who advise, prescribe or influence the buying of the product without ever purchasing it). Thus a babyfood manufacturer may have to evaluate the perceptions of babies (consumers), housewives (purchasers), supermarkets (distributors) and doctors (specifiers). A floor tile company might be concerned with householders (consumers) and builders' merchants (distributors) in one segment and local authorities (purchasers), contractors (customers), and architects (specifiers) in another.

Statistically valid samples of each of the relevant groups should be identified and asked to specify their needs or purchasing criteria in priority order. This may require the use of a prompting list. The respondents are then requested to rank the competitive offerings in terms of how well they satisfy their requirements.

The example shown in Table 3.1 from the financial advisory market has been chosen to demonstrate that this technique is applicable in services as well as consumer and industrial product marketing.

Furthermore, the assessments obtained cover not only the relative

Table 3.1
Perception survey questionnaire – financial advisory services

The object of this survey was to identify how the various segments of the market (merchant banks, unit trusts, investment houses, pension funds and insurance companies) perceived their own needs for guidance on investment analysis and how they rated the performance of various stock-brokers (including our client) in supplying them. Some of the main questions are listed below.

Q. 1	Which sources do you use for investment analysis?
Q. 2	(If answers to Q.1 are vague, prompt by) Do you use – your own sources? 　　　　　 – industry contacts? 　　　　　 – your broker? 　　　　　 – others?
Q. 3	Of the sources mentioned which do you use most often?
Q. 4	How many brokers do you use for investment analysis?
Q. 5	Which sectors of the stock market are of most interest?
Q. 6	Which individual companies are of most interest?
Q. 7	Which sectors of the stock market do you regard as: 　　over-researched? 　　under-researched?
Q. 8	What information is necessary but unavailable from brokers?
Q. 9	Which sectors do you associate with the following brokers? (List of ten named stockbrokers provided.)
Q.10	How would you rate them on their investment analysis? (List of brokers and six-point scale from excellent to very poor provided.)
Q.11	Are there any brokers not named to whom you would give an excellent or good rating?
Q.12	Ideally, what type of service do you want from brokers?
Q.13	(If answers to Q.12 are vague, prompt by) Do you want – 'phone contact with salesman? 　　　　　 – 'phone contact with analyst? 　　　　　 – visits from salesman? 　　　　　 – visits to the broker? 　　　　　 – any other?
Q.14	Which services do you get from those brokers you use?
Q.15	Which factors significantly influence your decision in selecting or rejecting brokers?
Q.16	How would you rate the following brokers on the services they render? (List of ten brokers provided.)

performance of the products or services of the firm, but also the marketing activity supporting the products or services. Thus an overall picture can be gained of the effectiveness of all the elements in the marketing mix.

By assessing each component in the market system and comparing the results, problems of conflict within the system may be identified, for instance, as often occurs between distributors and consumers. The manufacturer must be able to weigh the competitive advantage of, for example, lower prices to the consumer against the competitive disadvantage of lower profits to the distributor. In one case a manufacturer of DIY equipment discovered that his policy of factory after-sales service direct to the consumer, which was perceived by the market (and his own marketing team) as a major competitive 'plus', was seen as a disadvantage by the distributors as it reduced their profit potential. This had not been critical when unit sales volume was increasing, but as the market became saturated, the distributors wanted to be able to participate in the lucrative parts and service business. This example demonstrates not only the importance of comparing the needs of the various levels in the market system, but also how such needs can alter with changing market circumstances.

The needs of the company

The corporate marketing activity has to satisfy not only the needs of the marketplace but also the requirements of the firm. Key criteria therefore need to be defined to evaluate how well it is performing in this regard. Many such standards should already be specified in the company plans and budgets. Targets of profit, sales by revenue and volume, margins, market share and promotional expenditure can all be used to appraise marketing performance and are particularly valuable when broken down by product, market segment and region. This then allows detailed examination which can identify relative strengths and weaknesses within the activity. Why is one product succeeding better than another? What is causing higher sales performance in one territory relative to another? Of course answering such questions is an integral part of the management task; the function of the audit is to investigate in greater depth than may be possible for operating managers because of their daily pressures. Such investigations may take the form of deeper analysis of present performance relative to the past or comparisons with other similar marketing activities, such as different divisions within the company or comparable firms in the same industry. These comparisons are often based on management ratio analysis starting from the basic profit mechanism:

$$\frac{\text{Return (usually net profit before tax)}}{\substack{\text{Capital employed} \\ \text{(Fixed assets + current assets} \\ \text{− current liabilities)}}} = \frac{\text{Return}}{\text{Sales}} \times \frac{\text{Sales}}{\text{Capital employed}}$$

Each of the secondary ratios can be further analysed; the R/S figure in terms of volume, price, mix and cost, the S/CE in terms of the relationship

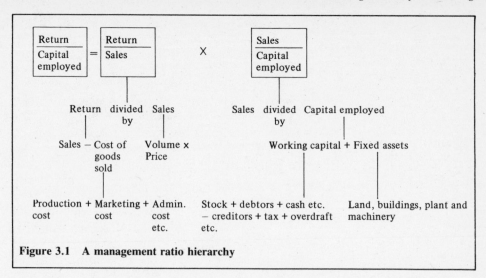

Figure 3.1   A management ratio hierarchy

between sales and the fixed assets (land, buildings, plant machinery etc.) and between sales and working capital (current assets such as stock, debtors, work in progress etc., minus current liabilities such as creditors, tax, overdrafts etc.). Thus a hierarchy of ratios can be developed as shown in Figure 3.1. As most of the key figures are available from published balance sheets and profit and loss accounts, it is possible to compare companies using this technique. Organizations such as Inter Company Comparisons Ltd and Dun and Bradstreet publish industry comparisons and the Centre for Interfirm Comparison accepts commissions from groups of companies who wish to assess their performance while remaining anonymous. The same method can apply of course to the comparison within a single firm of one year against another, or one division against another. Although not all the ratios are of equal relevance to marketing evaluation, most of them contribute to the assessment of marketing performance. Some of the key marketing ratios are listed in Table 3.2.

The ratios themselves, of course, do not define what is an acceptable level of performance; such criteria need to be specified from the goals, plans and budgets of the company, past results or an analysis of the performance of the industry.

Having evaluated the needs of the various levels in the market system and how well they are currently being satisfied, and having established how far the requirements of the firm are being met in terms of profit, sales, market share and other goals, we can now examine in more detail the auditing of the four main elements of the marketing operation: the product offering, pricing, distribution and promotion activities. As the Preface made clear, this book does not attempt to cover all the techniques and methods involved in these tactical areas. There are plenty of excellent texts on them, some of which are recommended in the booklist at the end of this volume. The objective of the following discussion is to identify from our experience the key factors that the Marketing Director should check and suggest how they may be evaluated.

Table 3.2
Seven key questions for diagnosing declining profitability

Question	Measurement
Question	*Measurement*
1 Is profitability falling?	$\dfrac{R}{CE}$
2 To what is this due?	$\dfrac{R}{S}$ or $\dfrac{S}{CE}$
3 If $\dfrac{R}{S}$ what could be the changes in one or a combination of causes?	– unit volume (V) – price (P) – costs (C) – mix (M)
4 If it is a change in the interrelationships, how can it be identified?	Price change $\dfrac{\text{S by product}}{\text{V by product}}$ (average price per product group) Mix change $\dfrac{\text{S by product}}{\text{S in total}}$ (% sales accounted for by each product group) Cost/volume change $\dfrac{S-R}{V}$ (cost of goods sold)
5 If falling profitability is due however to $\dfrac{S}{CE}$ what could be the causes?	$\dfrac{S}{\text{Fixed assets}}$ or $\dfrac{S}{\text{Working capital}}$
6 If $\dfrac{S}{FA}$ what are the likely reasons?	Either under-utilization (utilized capacity as % of total capacity) or new fixed assets not yet producing a return $\dfrac{\text{Fixed assets}}{\text{Total assets}}$ as %
7 If $\dfrac{S}{WC}$ what are the likely reasons?	Either $\dfrac{\text{Sales}}{\text{Stocks}}$ or $\dfrac{\text{Sales}}{\text{Debtors}}$ or $\dfrac{\text{Sales}}{\text{Work in progress}}$

The product offering

Good products or services are obviously essential to the continuing prosperity of the company. It is therefore important to assess fully, relative to competition, their current performance in terms of the needs they aim to satisfy and the future development programme.

Again, the evaluation should start with the consumers to ensure that the marketplace concept of the product is fully recognized by the company.

Every marketing executive recognizes that products are bought for what they do rather than what they are; that the benefits conferred by the product are created not only from its actual physical features, but also from a whole constellation of other objective and subjective characteristics such as availability, reputation, after-sales service etc. The review of the competitive position of current products should try to evaluate which particular aspects are of prime importance to the marketplace, both at consumer and distributor level. All too often we find that the products and the services surrounding them have over the years been modified by internal company requirements such as production or financial constraints, often at the same time as the market needs were evolving too. The product audit may thus reveal a degree of mismatch between the company offering and the marketplace with the company placing emphasis on product aspects which are of little consumer or retailer interest. This affects not only sales volumes, but also profitability because the costs of creating the product offering are not related to the benefits gained by the purchaser, which of course is what determines the price he is willing to pay.

A value analysis approach is useful here to evaluate the relationship between costs and benefits. In one case it was demonstrated that the expensive diecast chromium plated handle on bathroom weighing scales added significantly to the cost but little to the value because it was shown that consumers do not in fact need to carry the scales very often. The handle had been added originally 'because the competitors had one'! Its removal did not reduce the product's consumer appeal but created the possibility of profit increase or price reduction. In another company the parts supply service for maintenance and repair of the firm's capital equipment products was speeded up so that parts could be supplied within 12 instead of 24 hours. The majority of the customers, however, did not require the quicker service as they kept small stocks of replacement parts themselves and their maintenance schedules allowed for a 24-hour delivery. The increasing of the service thus added to the cost without making a concomitant increase in its value.

Assessing whether the product offering still matches the needs it was designed to satisfy competitively and cost-effectively can also help identify its position in its life cycle. Although the concept of the product life cycle appears somewhat theoretical to many Marketing Directors, especially those in non-branded industrial products, the causes that produce life cycles should be evaluated in any review of the current product range. Consumer needs can and do change albeit in some industries over a long time; the means by which those needs can be satisfied also evolve. Even where it seems impractical to attempt to plot life cycles for the products, it is worth listing the opportunities and threats they face from social, economic, technological and competitive change, and identifying what, if anything, the company can and should do.

The current products should also be reviewed as a range, both externally and internally. Many managements believe that they must offer a complete range to their markets; in some firms it has become almost a tenet of faith to be 'a full product line company'. This is usually justified on the basis of the needs of the consumers and distributors in general, or in particular, that customer X will not buy product A unless he can also have product Z. The evidence from the marketplace seldom justifies the managerial belief. Industry is perfectly prepared to buy computers from one company and the software to go with them from another; farmers will purchase tractors from one agricultural machinery supplier and the implements they tow from another; consumers will buy different brands of record players, amplifiers and loud speakers and create their own stereo systems.

The problem of the full line manufacturer is that usually he cannot possess the resources of R and D, finance, production, marketing and management to compete effectively with all the specialist suppliers who can each concentrate on a more limited product range and thus better serve those particular consumer needs. Distributors, too, often prefer not to buy a whole product range from a single manufacturer because it can make them vulnerable to commercial pressure, production breakdown or strikes. Objective assessment of consumer and distributor preferences and attitudes is needed to decide whether the current range is appropriate. Although this will usually suggest the current range is too large, we have had cases where such studies have demonstrated not only the relationship between products showing that elimination of one would certainly affect sales of another, but also extensions in the product range which would be welcomed by the market.

In one company supplying castings for rock and ore crushing plants the elimination of apparently unprofitable products was being considered on the assumption that the products were regarded independently by the market. Research showed however that customers not only wanted to purchase lining plates and grinding media from the same supplier, but also even simple ancillary items such as nuts, bolts and packing material which our client did not supply. This desire for a fuller range had developed because crushing plants tended to be located near the rock or ore sources often in remote areas of the Third World and the installation and maintenance of such plants was considerably easier and less costly if all the products necessary could be purchased and shipped as a package deal from one supplier. This suggested that our client should in fact extend his range, rather than reduce it if he was to satisfy customer needs more effectively and profitably.

Internal evaluation of the product range usually commences with a sales and profitability analysis of each product and the contribution it makes to the total range.* This often shows an 80:20 relationship, i.e. that 80 per cent of the sales (and often more of the profit) is generated by only 20 per cent of the products. Conversely 80 per cent of the products produce only 20 per cent of the results and it is the worst performers in this group that need urgent review. We have often found that the bottom 5 per cent or so

---

*There are a number of techniques of categorization or 'portfolio analysis' as it is sometimes called. Probably the best known is the approach originated by Boston Consulting Group which groups products (or businesses within large companies) into 'stars' (those with high market share in high growth markets), 'questionmarks' (low share in high growth markets) 'cash cows' (high share in low growth markets) and 'dogs' (low share in low growth markets).

produce very few sales and in fact make losses, even on product costing systems which do not attempt to allocate all the overhead expenditure. In reality the cost of such products is even higher than shown because ironically it is usually such products that occupy a great deal of management time and attention. It almost appears as if the 80:20 rule works in reverse with 80 per cent of the management time being spent on products which at best can only achieve 20 per cent of the results!

Costly products need to be evaluated to see whether anything can be done to improve sales or profits, and if not, what will be the effect on other products if they are discontinued. As has already been said, such effects are usually exaggerated by management and thus external evidence is required. Elimination of such products can be very significant as it tends to release disproportionate productive, financial and managerial capacity.

In addition to reviewing the current product range, the audit should also evaluate the product development programme at least to ensure that it is a continuous and systematic process. If products go through a life cycle of introduction, growth, maturity and decline there must be a steady flow of new products at least on the same time-scale if the company is to maintain a growth pattern. Moreover, because the failure rate of new products is high (up to 70 per cent within the first year in some fast-moving consumer goods industries), the whole process of evolving ideas, screening, development, test-marketing and launching needs to be given top management attention. One important factor, in our experience, is to ensure that regardless of the origin of the idea (e.g. from technical research, production capability or even management creativity!) there is a proven genuine, albeit latent market need and that the new product is evaluated regularly against that need throughout the development process. This is because all too often either the need itself changes or the product veers away from the original concept during the development process. The result is the wrong product in the wrong market at the wrong time – the key ingredients of disasters like the Edsel.

The second important factor is the amount of management attention that is given to new products, particularly during the introductory period; as the new product comes into the range, the marketing team must make sure that the everyday pressures from the rest of the existing business do not detract from the additional effort that is needed to push the product into its growth phase, particularly by widening its distribution.

Reviewing the pricing approach, policy and structure

The reality of pricing strategy and tactics is often far from textbook descriptions as most Marketing Directors will acknowledge. This is because of the difficulty of isolating price as a variable and assessing the reactions to price change in other than commodity markets. Price demand theory says that demand will increase as price is lowered and vice versa, all other factors being equal. Of course, with most products and services, all other things are not equal and management teams devote much attention to trying to create differences by product development, branding, publicity etc. In reality, the cheapest product or service is seldom the market leader, although the dearest often is, in fields as diverse as computers and car hire. This raises the question of the concept of price in the purchaser's mind because obviously no buyer wishes to pay more than he or she needs for the values sought. Those values, however, cannot be easily quantified as they include not only measurable factors such as product specification, performance, support services, but also the qualitative aspects of brand loyalty, status, prestige, security etc. The product audit should have given some definition to the company's offering *vis-à-vis* competition across the whole range of values, and this can be used to evaluate the relative price levels. Some companies attempt to rate and weight each factor in the total offering and compare themselves against competition to provide a basis for price setting. A motor manufacturer, for instance, might list all the features of a car and allocate a number of points to each. The manufacturer then scores his own car against competition, often using consumer research to provide an objective basis of information. If his car scores 100 against one competitor at 90 and another at 105, he will position his price between them accordingly. The problem of such systems is not in identifying the relative importance of the product features, nor in assessing which competitor offers the best performance per feature. It is in quantifying how much each feature is worth, both absolutely and relatively (as obviously they are not sold separately). Thus while it may be shown quite clearly, for example, that seating capacity is more important than boot capacity, it is impossible to prove that one is worth £3x, the other only £2x. The problem is further magnified when attempting to rate subjective factors such as design, comfort or image. Despite these drawbacks, at least such methods offer a systematic approach to consumer price evaluation.

In industrial marketing, price is often perceived as the key factor by the marketing team in general and the sales force in particular. While we do not deny its importance, it is our experience that it is usually overrated. Industry does not buy on price alone; again there is a number of subjective factors that must be considered as in consumer marketing, although of course the factors are different. For example, the inertia of buyers can be demonstrated in that it takes a price change of some magnitude to cause most buyers to change suppliers and typically a well-established manufacturer will not be replaced automatically by slightly cheaper competition, even though the buyer, for negotiating reasons, might threaten the salesman with losing the business if prices are increased.

A philosophy of market-related pricing provides the only valid long-term approach, difficult though it is to quantify, and should be the basis of the pricing policy. The degree of price sensitivity in the market should also be assessed, i.e. how sales react to price changes. This is affected by the frequency of change, and in highly inflationary environments, like Britain in the late '70s, both consumer and industrial awareness tends to be reduced.

Because inflation, devaluation, floating currencies and dramatic cost changes in both absolute and relative terms affect both purchasers and suppliers, it is valuable to audit the whole pricing approach of the company, examining such questions as:

1   *What is the basis of pricing policy? Is it market-related (as described above), cost-plus or follow-the-competition?*

Cost-plus pricing is still very common and at least defines minimum levels below which it is not profitable to sell. However, it fails to recognize values perceived by the purchaser if they do not feature in the costing system, such as confidence created by the past performance of the company. Setting prices in line with competition again is a frequent approach, but unless it is done as described above in the motor industry, it can lead to price wars where the purchaser is led to conclude that the only difference between competing offerings is price. This led to disaster in the package holiday business with the industry as a whole making a net loss in particularly bad years.

2   *Is there a sensible pricing structure? Are the various products in the range appropriately differentiated? Are the needs of both the company and the distributive network reflected in the trade margin structure? Does the discount structure reflect true cost savings or volume gains?*

Pricing structures in many companies have not been kept in line with the changing environment or modifications in the activities of the firm. Those companies which sell through distribution networks should evaluate their pricing structures very carefully. The distributor's prime need is to make profits, which is basically a function of the margin that he makes multiplied by his volume of sales. The manufacturer's goal is usually to increase sales through his distributors. Where the manufacturer sets low prices to the distributor in the hope that the increased margin will encourage the distributor to stock and sell more, he may find that the distributor either uses the extra margin to discount the price to the end-user (often causing a price war which then leads to the demand for further increases in margin) or retains the extra margin which can mean that he can achieve his profit goal on a lower sales volume (exactly the opposite effect to that which the manufacturer intended).

In evaluating distributor pricing policy and structure, the Marketing Director must check whether the policy takes into account:

1   The present consumer price that the company would like to see charged (even though there are few countries now where resale prices can be enforced).
2   The volume of sales and stock turn that the distributor should achieve.
3   The costs of handling and promoting the products that the distributor should incur.
4   The return on investment that the distributor is trying to make.
5   The cost of servicing the distributor.

The company's discount structure (quantity discounts, early settlement discounts, annual rebates, etc.) should be reviewed to check that it reflects true cost savings or sales gains. In our experience it is common to find that the discount structure has not been changed to reflect changing circumstances; the examples in Chapter 2 of discount structures which failed to reflect current transport fleet capacities or palletization are not isolated. Early settlement discounts given to late payers and rebates still allowed when targets have been missed are also often found.

In one food company we were asked to investigate why, despite adding many new products from both development and acquisition, total sales were only increasing very slowly, and the new product sales seemed to be partially at the expense of sales of existing products. We discovered that the quantity discount structure was based on the total number of cases ordered and the levels at which extra discount became payable had not been changed for years. Therefore, the buyer who had become accustomed to purchasing say 1000 cases per week and thus gaining a certain level of discount, was simply dividing his order over an increasing number of products, thus reducing the sales of some of the established lines.

3   *Within the general policy and structure what are the pricing strategies of the company? Does it use penetration pricing (setting lower prices to achieve higher sales, enter new markets, fight competition, establish high market share) or premium pricing (accepting lower sales but higher margins, thus creating finance for more aggressive marketing and/or increased profits)? Is the appropriate strategy used for relevant products, market segments or different geographic markets?*

We have sometimes found lack of congruence between the pricing strategy and the company's capacities as, for example, in the luxury car market where there have been several cases of manufacturers setting price levels which generated awareness and demand far higher than they could supply, thus opening the door to competition. The fact that these cars commanded a higher price in the secondhand market demonstrates a lack of awareness of consumer value:price perception which perhaps led to the wrong choice of strategy.

Pricing may stil be more of an art than science and an art that has not been made any easier by the rapidly changing environment affecting both purchasers and suppliers. Regular audits of pricing policy, structure and strategy are important to ensure that they are up-to-date and that the profitability of the company is maintained. Government price regulation is a constant threat in so many countries and we have seen a number of companies trapped in anachronistic levels and structures by such legislation.

Evaluating the distribution activity

The rapidly evolving patterns of distribution on both a national and international scale were highlighted in Chapter 2 as a key factor of the environment in which the company must operate. The marketing audit should assess the corporate performance in terms of the effectiveness of current distribution strategy, outlet management activities and physical distribution.

Distribution strategy

The distribution strategy should have defined 'how can the products be best got to market' which in turn is derived from the corporate marketing decisions on which markets are to be served by which products. There are four aspects of the distribution strategy that should be evaluated:

1 *Is the desired market access being achieved?*

This means reviewing the existing network coverage against the chosen market segments to check that the selected groups of consumers can be reached by the distribution channels used. This may involve studying the catchment areas of the outlets concerned, as well as making sure that no new channels have developed and taken custom away from the company's traditional distribution. In one case, working with a consumer durable manufacturer, we identified that his policy of increasingly selective distribution was excluding him from a larger percentage of the market than he had calculated, although his market share goals and his publicity campaigns were based tacitly on the whole market being available.

In another example, the policy of a sports goods company specified that their products would only be sold through specialist sports equipment outlets, thus failing to recognize the product range extension happening in other networks such as photographic and electronic equipment stores as they evolved towards supplying the total leisure market.

2 *Are the current outlets giving appropriate consumer service?*

This implies that the manufacturer has consumer service level criteria for his outlets in terms of product availability in range and depth of stock, technical advice and after-sales service where appropriate, credit and payment terms, etc. Of all these, stock availability is probably the most important, because unless the product is readily available when the consumer wants it, in most product categories the shopper will choose an obtainable alternative. Related to the consumer service levels are the outlet service standards that are demanded from the manufacturer. These cover order size and shape (e.g. pallet load), items per order, order cycle and frequency, mode of transport, terms and conditions of payment etc. Again the critical factor is usually the manufacturer's performance in making the product available.

However, the Marketing Director should check the relationship between stocks held in the outlet and his own delivery system. One of our clients changed his delivery system from weekly to thrice weekly to give a better service to his outlets, albeit at a considerable cost to himself which he hoped to recover from the additional sales generated. However, the retailers quickly realized that they need not carry as much stock with such frequent delivery which meant, that they were out of stock more often and sales suffered.

Finally, the relationship between the number of outlets, the forecast sales per outlet and the total supply capability should be examined. If a manufacturer has too many outlets relative to his production capacity, inevitably no outlet will have enough stock to sell. The distributors will rapidly lose interest and switch their attention to other products as happened with a furniture manufacturer who could not supply consumer demand, particularly through the multiplicity of outlets he had. Most furniture sales take place on Saturdays and it is common in the trade to have part-time commission-only Saturday salesmen. They rapidly learnt that if they sold this manufacturer's product, they had to wait for their commission because of the very long delivery delays. They were therefore much more motivated to sell whatever else was available. As the majority of brand decisions can be influenced at the point of sales by the salesman, they were therefore highly successful in persuading consumers not to buy from the manufacturer with production limitations. Furthermore, they went on selling other brands long after this manufacturer's products, not surprisingly, came into freer supply!

The problem of reconciling consumer demand with production output is of course a perennial one, but at least the company should ensure that its distribution strategy does not exacerbate it. Rather than risk alienating most of the consumers and most of the outlets for most of the time, it is usually better to limit strategically the number of outlets so that at least each of them can satisfy their consumers while making profitable business for themselves.

3   What is the balance of power between manufacturer and distributor?

A useful way to evaluate this is to calculate what percentage of business is held by each network and in some cases by individual outlets and compare it with the percentage of the distributor's business that is taken by the manufacturer. Some companies specify the maximum percentage of their business that they will allow to be held by any one outlet and/or network. On the other hand if the business is spread across too many outlets, the manufacturer may not be important enough to any one distributor to justify much attention. Again some manufacturers specify a minimum amount or a percentage of the outlet's business that they wish to occupy in order to be of significance.

For example, one industrial component manufacturer selects the distributors with whom he wishes to trade on the basis of the position of his product category within the distributor's total business and the share that he can expect of that product category. The current criteria are that the product category should be about 20 per cent of the total and he aims for 80 per cent share of that 20 per cent, thus representing about 16 per cent of the distributor's total volume which is a significant portion for both parties.

These standards were defined from a study of the alternatives; the manufacturer had found that where the product category represented much more than 20 per cent of the distributor's business, the distributor tended to divide his business across more competitor brands in order to protect himself against manufacturer pressure or failure to supply, thus making it difficult for our client to achieve a high share. Conversely, where the product category was much below 20 per cent, although a high share could be gained, this portion of the distributor business became relatively insignificant and was given little attention.

4 *Does the current distribution strategy give significant competitive advantage?*

This may mean attempting to gain exclusive franchises or choosing different networks from competition. One slimming products company achieved a successful competitive edge by selling through chemists only, thus gaining the backing of that trade against competitive suppliers who sell through grocery outlets as well. In some industries, such as tyres, agricultural merchanting, DIY products and electronic equipment, manufacturers have sought to win competitive advantage by buying or establishing their own distributive networks. In such cases, distribution policy and practice needs very careful review. The essence of retailing either consumer or industrial products is that the range stocked and sold must reflect the needs of the consumers to be served. If the manufacturer having bought the retailer tries to exclude competitive products and replace them with his own out of all proportion to the market requirements, the retailer will begin to fail in his basic function. Furthermore, if the manufacturer treats his own outlets not as he would a customer but as a department of his own company, again problems are likely to occur.

For example, as part of a study for a leisure equipment manufacturer, we visited anonymously a number of retail outlets, including some that he owned but under a different name, to ascertain which products were emphasized by the store assistants and why. Paradoxically we discovered that in the manufacturer-owned outlets his own products received the least sales attention; in some cases our researchers were warned off them! The reason, we subsequently discovered, was that the manufacturer did not treat his own outlets as customers and gave priority of delivery, stock, literature, advice and support to the independent outlets. This had resulted in a lack of stock and information about his own products in his own outlets which had motivated the sales assistants to sell competitive brands about which they felt more knowledgeable and confident and which they knew they could deliver.

Outlet management activities

Outlet management activities include the selection (and where appropriate the legal or quasi-legal appointment) of distribution outlets, developing and supporting them and monitoring their performance. Some of these activities will normally be performed by the sales force, others by various marketing functions, such as brand or product management, advertising and sales promotion, specialist distribution development departments or trade managers.

1 *Have the outlets been correctly selected and appointed?*

The first step in checking is to ensure that the outlets being used match the criteria defined in the distribution strategy, i.e. they are the right type of outlet, in the right place, with the right business profile and characteristics, and that there is the right number of them. This is particularly important in export markets where having the appropriate outlets, distributors or agents is often the key to success. However, we find that many manufacturers do not pay sufficient attention to the selection and appointment of overseas distribution outlets as was evidenced in the examples in Chapter 2 of companies being locked into unsatisfactory agreements or facing large compensation claims.

Every Marketing Director would be wise to check his distributor arrangements or agreements from time to time if only to discover what his predecessors have committed him to! In one large international company we found fourteen different forms of dealer agreements in operation in various markets with no other explanation than they had been made at different times by different managers and many of them were totally unsatisfactory in the light of the company's current policy and operations.

2   *Are the outlets being given sufficient support and development?*

Most companies now recognize that if they are to achieve results in an increasingly competitive environment, they must *market through* their distribution channels, not simply *sell to* them. This means supporting the outlet, whether retail shop, industrial dealer or franchised distributor, by creating consumer demand and helping develop the efficiency of the business. What kind of support is appropriate varies according to the industry, and the distribution network. In evaluating this aspect of the marketing activity, the Marketing Director should start by analysing the problems and opportunities of his distributors' businesses to identify where support can and should be given. Basically a distributive outlet consists of facilities (warehouse, shop, workshop, materials handling equipment etc.), systems (order handling, invoicing, stock planning and control) and people (management and staff in sales, purchasing, finance, the warehouse etc.), and help may be required in any or all of these areas.

Some manufacturers provide advice and even financial assistance to improve the facilities such as refurbishing the premises, erecting better signs etc. The brewery industry is very active in this way. Others provide systems support; one Swedish tool company has allowed its dealers to have remote access terminals linked to the manufacturer's computer so that they can improve their order placing, stock planning and profitability analysis. At the same time this puts the manufacturer into a powerful position *vis-à-vis* both the distributors and competitive suppliers. Another example of systems support is the computerized shelf planning service we developed with the toy company mentioned earlier.

Management and staff training is a problem for many distributive outlets which tend to have relatively few staff and a large number of product lines. Product training is of course commonplace (but can often be improved); we have constructed training programmes with many manufacturers to help develop distributive management and staff in sales techniques, sales management, financial planning and control, promotion, stock management, etc., in such diverse industries as frozen food wholesaling, agricultural machinery distributors, motor dealers and franchised hotels.

3   *Is outlet performance being regularly assessed?*

The monitoring and control of distributive outlets is the key to effective distribution outlet management. The first step is to evaluate the performance of the outlet against the criteria laid down in the distribution policy and strategy. This involves for many manufacturers a development of their accounting systems to enable costs to be allocated by distributive network and outlet, especially the major accounts. We find that in many companies although costs can be allocated by cost centre or product group they cannot be identified by customer, which limits the monitoring and control process. When the exercise is undertaken and profit and loss accounts for major customers produced, it is often discovered, to the manufacturer's horror, that he is actually losing money on supplying his major outlets! Even where this is not the case, the customer profit and loss account generally gives a good basis for successful future negotiations. We have developed these techniques, sometimes computerized, for companies in a variety of industries, for example, food, consumer electronics and domestic appliances.

The monitoring and control process is much broader than checking results against targets or producing major customer profit and loss accounts. Control must be maintained to ensure the selected networks are giving the desired market access and consumer service, that no one outlet is growing too powerful (with inevitably long-term painful results for the manufacturer), that competition is not gaining advantage in the outlets or in other networks (often the strategy employed by foreign competition breaking into a market), and that the manufacturer's total service (sales, delivery, techical, etc.) is continuing to satisfy the distribution outlet.

This long-term network maintenance process can help solve some of the fundamental problems caused in the later stages of the distribution system life cycle. For example, some companies run 'dealer's sons' training programmes to ensure management succession; others help finance young entrepreneurs to establish new distributive outlets and thus rejuvenate the system. Yet others establish their own outlets in areas where the network is moribund or where there are gaps, thus gaining first-hand valuable distributive management experience which can be applied to the independent outlets in the network.

Checking the physical distribution system

The main decisions involved in physical distribution management from the manufacturer's point of view are what stocks to hold, where, and how to transport them from the factory to the warehouses, and from there to the distributive outlets. These questions can only be sensibly answered on the basis of clear and specific marketing and distribution policies and strategies. Given a statement of which markets are to be served by which distributive outlets in what volumes and at what consumer and distributor service levels, it is not too difficult to assess what stocks should be held where. However, because of the lack of a total distribution concept and the fragmentation of responsibility in most companies, decisions about physical distribution tend to be taken without full regard to the broader marketing implications. Therefore the physical distribution system should be evaluated in the light of the following questions.

1   *Is the appropriate stock available?*

The balancing of sales and production demands, of course, close congruence between sales forecasting, sales control, stock planning and production scheduling within the context of clear marketing and distribution strategies. Furthermore, this may require reallocation of management responsibilities in some companies and physical relocation of departments to improve communications. Distributors need availability of product or failing that, reliable information on when availability can be expected. In a study of customer complaints about wrong or non-delivery for a tableware manufacturer we found that although communications with the distributive outlets were good (i.e. prompt and helpful), the information given often turned out to be wrong, largely because the sales office handling complaints was on one site, the dispatch office on another and the warehouse on a third.

2   *Are the warehousing arrangements satisfactory?*

Because of the absence of clear policies and strategies in many companies, physical distribution management is often left with no alternative but to attempt to be as efficient as possible within the existing system. In such circumstances the numbers, locations and sizes of warehouses tend to be taken as fixed and efforts made to optimize performance within their constraints. This seems illogical when it can be clearly seen that markets are changing in nature, scale and often location, that distribution networks are evolving, products are changing and the lead times for putting a warehouse in operation are lengthening. However, in many of the original briefs we are given to review warehousing operations, there is the tacit assumption that today's market and distributive environment will continue indefinitely. Thus in an assignment for a European office machinery client, we were originally asked to recommend improvements to the operation of the central warehouse within the context of the existing market and distributive system. A deeper investigation of the changing environment demonstrated clearly that the real problem was that the warehouse was now in the wrong place.

3   *Is the transport system efficient?*

Too often it seems that transport decisions are taken in isolation, e.g. how much will it cost? how long will it take? These are of course important questions, but certainly no more important than ensuring that the transport function meets the criteria for the total distribution activity. For example, in one food company we investigated, where the marketing strategy was to sell and service wholesale and retail outlets separately, delivery to the outlets was combined on the same trucks although the order characteristics of the two types of outlet were incompatible in terms of order size and frequency of delivery.

In another firm, small loads were being delayed until they could be aggregated as the haulier had imposed minimum charges, apparently a reasonable management decision. However, many of the small loads were parts of larger orders for major customers that the company had failed to deliver previously because they had been out of stock or the truck had been full. From the customer's point of view, it was annoying enough that part of the order had not been delivered the first time; for it to be delayed longer than necessary was infuriating. In such a case, the transport department can hardly be criticized; given no other guidance, it simply operated as efficiently as possible within the constraints of stock availability, truck size and transport costs.

It can even happen that the very enthusiasm and apparent efficiency of the transport department can detrimentally affect the achievement of the manufacturer's marketing objectives by giving too good a service. In one company we investigated, the transport department provided a national 4-hour delivery service to retailers, obviously at considerable cost. This encouraged the retailers to carry very low stocks and therefore actually reduced the chances of immediate availability to the consumer. Competitive manufacturers on the other hand provided a less frequent delivery service (at lower cost) which motivated the retailers to carry higher stocks and thus gave better in-store availability.

CHECKLIST

1 *The perception survey*

1.1 Have we identified clearly enough the various groups we are aiming to satisfy (e.g. consumers, purchasers, distributors, customers, specifiers)?

1.2 Have we checked objectively the satisfactions they require?

1.3 Do we know how well our total offering (i.e. the product/price/ promotion package) is currently satisfying their needs?

1.4 Do we know how well competitive offerings are satisfying those needs?

2 *The needs of the company*

2.1 Is there a clear definition of how the marketing activity should contribute to the profit mechanism of the firm?

2.2 Does the marketing management team understand the financial mechanism?

2.3 Are we using management ratios as a tool to diagnose the strengths and weaknesses of our financial performance?

2.4 Do we compare our financial performance against other divisions or other companies to identify areas for improvement?

3 *The present and future product offering*

3.1 Do the current products match the current needs of the various groups in the market system cost-effectively?

3.2 Do we know where they stand on their life cycles?

3.3 Have we evaluated the product range recently?

3.4 Is the product development process fully effective?

4 *Pricing approach, policy and structure*

4.1 Do we have a systematic approach to market-related pricing?

4.2 Is our pricing fully up to date in the light of inflation, currency fluctuations, etc?

4.3 Do we have a logical and up-to-date pricing structure?

4.4 Are appropriate pricing strategies being used for different markets and/or product groups?

5 *Distribution activity*

5.1 Does our current distribution strategy give the desired market access and customer service levels?

5.2 Have we considered deeply enough the changing balance of power *vis-à-vis* the distribution networks, outlets and competition?

5.3 Are we supporting and controlling the outlets sufficiently?

5.4 Is our physical distribution system kept in line with changing markets and company activities?

Chapter 4

The Marketing Audit – 2

Evaluating the promotional mix

The promotional mix of the firm embraces all the forms of communication that can be or are being used to influence the various elements of the market system – consumers or end-users, distributors and/or customers. Although there are dozens of different ways of communicating and influencing these target groups, they can be classified under the four headings of public relations, advertising, sales promotion and personal selling. Because most organizations use a variety of promotional activities at any one moment, the essential problem of evaluation is one of trying to identify what results have been caused by which action.

Every Marketing Director must have spent many hours attempting to decide how much of the sales volume is due to the advertising campaign as opposed to the other sales-creating influences. Rather than trying to isolate the effect of a single variable on the total result, it is often more practical and fruitful to review the total promotional task and the individual contribution that each category of techniques should be making towards achieving the objective of influencing the various elements in the market system. For example, it is the job of the sales force of a food company to influence the supermarket buyers, the role of advertising to convince potential consumers, the task of merchandising to ensure the product is persuasively displayed in-store. If any one fails, sales will not occur, therefore the other two also appear to fail if measured simply by results.

As sales cannot thus be used as a yardstick to measure any one type of promotional activity, the only valid criteria must be the particular goals of each individual category of techniques and the total results achieved by the mix of all of them.

There are two concepts from which models can be derived that are useful in evaluating the effectiveness of the total promotional mix and the role of the individual categories within it. The first concept is the perception of the total market mechanism between manufacturer and consumer in terms of buying and selling activities and influences. This helps define at which points promotional (i.e persuasive communication) activity should be directed. These points need further definition in terms of the needs for and attitudes to the corporate offering so that the nature of the promotional message can be specified. Figure 4.1 shows a simple example of such a model. (It will be noted that these diagrams can be derived from the market system maps described in Chapter 2.)

The second concept is the recognition of the nature of the persuasive communication process which can be specified as the changing of the perception of the receiver from, at its most basic, total unawareness of the product to an intention to buy it. Such a transition can be described as the movement from unawareness to awareness of the product, awareness to knowledge about the product, knowledge to conviction of its benefits, conviction to the act of purchasing.

Given such concepts of who needs to be persuaded of what and how such persuasion works in communication terms, the auditor is in a much better position to evaluate the appropriateness of the various promotional activities. One of the key differences between the promotional techniques is their ability to achieve the different communication objectives at different levels of cost-effectiveness. For example, advertising can create awareness or knowledge, in some cases, even conviction, and in direct response businesses, actual sales. Personal selling likewise can achieve all four communication goals. However, in an industry like office equipment, promoting by advertising alone would be highly unlikely to create sufficient sales because too few prospective customers would purchase without personal explanation and demonstration. Promoting by personal selling

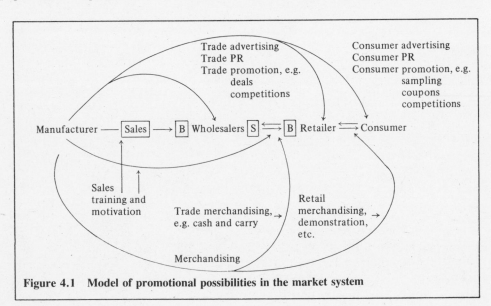

Figure 4.1   Model of promotional possibilities in the market system

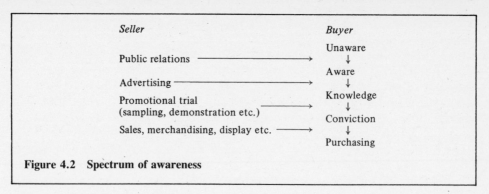

Figure 4.2   Spectrum of awareness

alone would be extremely expensive because a large number of the contacts, while being made well aware, knowledgeable, and even perhaps convinced, would not be ready, willing or able to purchase at the time of the call. Thus an appropriate cost-effective promotion mix could be to use advertising to create awareness and knowledge, sales promotions such as demonstrations and exhibitions to create conviction, reserving the high-cost technique of personal selling for closing the sale. Figure 4.2 shows the general relationship between the different communication objectives and the most cost-effective techniques of achieving them.

Using the two concepts of who needs to be persuaded of what and how the persuasion works, the Marketing Director can consider the relative contributions of the four major categories of promotional activity and the key factors that the audit should review.

Public relations

The objective of public relations activity is to create and maintain a favourable environment in which the company can operate. The environment can be defined as consisting of several groups of people: shareholders, government at local, national and even international level, present and prospective employees and suppliers, as well as consumers, distributors and customers. Because of this wide-ranging perspective, it is sometimes reasonably argued that PR is not simply a promotional tool for the marketing function. Here, however, we shall concentrate on its use within the marketing activity, although much of what is said will apply to its other roles.

To evaluate the appropriateness and then the effectiveness of PR, it is first necessary to define its target audience as precisely as possible. For example, if the general aim is at consumers, have certain groups of consumers been identified as particularly important – consumerists, future consumers, opinion formers amongst consumers, etc? Have such groups been specified in terms of who they are, how many people they consist of, what they do, read, listen to and see?

Further, what are the levels of knowledge, attitude and opinion of the target groups? If the aim of PR is to develop and maintain a favourable environment, this implies that without it the environment would be less favourable because of ignorance or prejudice. Furthermore, it implies that the company has defined what information in what presentation will create favourable attitudes and opinions towards it. Only when there is a clear concept of who should think what about the company and its activities can the message and methods of the PR activity be assessed for their relevance.

The same criteria should be used to evaluate the effectiveness of the PR activity, whatever the tactics used (e.g. press releases and conferences, sponsorship, factory visits, speeches to interested groups etc.). The success of PR activity should be measured in terms of the degree to which the target groups have gained awareness of and favourable attitudes towards the company.

In our experience, all too often there are no clearly defined goals for PR along the lines described above, so that the only assessment which can be and is made is in terms of coverage – column inches, numbers of articles, TV exposure etc. Whether the right people have now become better informed and more favourably inclined than they were before seems to be seldom investigated; thus the cost-effectiveness of the activity cannot be evaluated.

Advertising

This is a more powerful and controllable promotional weapon than PR because it is directly paid for by the company. It can therefore achieve more complex communication objectives, in some cases, such as direct response newspaper advertisements, taking the reader from unawareness to the point of purchase, in one act of persuasion. More usually it is employed to give knowledge about the product or service and to cause the reader, viewer or listener to remember, to think about, to examine or to try the product or service offered.

Within the context of the marketing audit, the evaluation of advertising relevance and effectiveness must again start from the definition of its communication goals – what should the target group think or do differently as a result of the campaign? Obviously this assumes that the target audiences have been specified with some exactitude in terms of their characteristics, notably their purchasing power and behaviour, and the media that have access to them. The message that is communicated and the way in which it is creatively expressed should be assessed against what is known of the target audiences' needs and attitudes and the competitive offerings.

Of course most companies delegate part or all of the often highly complex processes of creation of the advertisements and selection of the appropriate media to their advertising agencies. The auditor must check carefully that such delegation is not in fact abrogation by marketing management of their responsibilities for ensuring the appropriateness of the advertising within the total promotional mix.

An agency is seldom so well informed as the company about its total

marketing objectives, strategies and activities, and because of its special-
ization it can tend to see advertising as somewhat separate from, and often
more important than, other elements in the promotional mix. This is
perhaps hardly surprising when still the most common method of agency
remuneration is commission from the media. From the Marketing
Director's point of view, the agency should be treated like any other
department in his organization; it should be given a clear explanation of its
role and function within the corporate marketing objectives and strategies,
it should have its own goals agreed, its work should be planned, organized
and, in particular, monitored and controlled like any other marketing
section.

Such management of the agency can help ensure that appropriate
cost-effective advertising is produced because it will be fully integrated and
evaluated within the marketing background and activity. Sadly, this is
rarely the case, in our experience. For example, in auditing the marketing
plans of a bedding company, we reviewed the agency's proposals against the
company's and our knowledge and research of the market mechanisms, and
the other elements of the planned marketing mix. The agency was
proposing a campaign based on the girl lying in the bed in a typical retail
showroom with a message to the reader to try the product as she was doing.
The media recommendation was to concentrate on TV, particularly on
Friday evenings, backed by newspaper colour supplements with the names
of stores stocking the product, thus encouraging retailer support. Of
themselves, the recommendations seemed reasonable; the advertisements
were creatively constructed, the media were appropriate for the product
(showing retailers that they are being supported encouraged stocking).
However, the company had commissioned a consumer attitude study some
time before which demonstrated that the most embarrassing and distasteful
feature of the buying process for most purchasers was testing a bed in a shop
by lying on it. This raised serious doubts about the whole campaign theme
which both demonstrated and encouraged getting on to the bed, an act
perceived, as the research showed, as too intimate for public display.

Furthermore, a deeper consideration of purchasing behaviour revealed
illogicalities in the media recommendations. Most furniture purchasing
takes place on Saturdays, therefore TV advertising towards the end of the
week is likely to have most impact; but most newspaper colour supplements
appear on Sundays. Thus a campaign based on advertising on Friday to
encourage examination of the product on Saturday, but the whereabouts of
the product not being revealed until Sunday, was likely to confuse the
consumers and irritate the trade. The possible defence that the product was
in widespread distribution and that potential consumers would find it
anyway, had been unwittingly but effectively destroyed by the sale
department planning a programme of drastic reduction of the number of
outlets to be serviced to save distribution costs. Again, by itself, this had
seemed to be a well justified action programme. Not surprisingly the whole
marketing plan had to be reconsidered.

The case history highlights a number of key factors that need to be
reviewed in most companies when evaluating the advertising activity.

1   *Is the basic message that is being communicated likely to be persuasive to the target audience?*

Sometimes, management's subjective opinions (often based on their own needs and attitudes rather than those of their consumers) are given far too much weight. Also, it can happen that the agency's enthusiasm or the creativity or the novelty of the idea can bias its assessment. Certainly it has been shown that clients and agencies became bored much more quickly with their own advertising than do the audiences at whom it is directed. This causes campaigns to be changed too frequently, which however stimulating for the advertisers can be totally confusing for the market.

Confusion also results from the temptation which overtakes many managements to include every possible argument for their product in their advertisements. For example, an industrial subsidiary of a well-known major group launched its first consumer branded product which it then heavily advertised, sometimes with the stress on the brand name, at other times on the company name and at yet others on the group name. It thus hoped to gain the advantages of a strong brand identification, plus the development of a company reputation on which future consumer products could be introduced, plus additional benefit from the group corporate image which was already well known. Later research showed, however, that although the brand was now well recognized, consumers had been so confused by all the names that 80 per cent had assumed that such a good product must be made by the major competitor who was already established in this consumer market!

2   *Are the media selected appropriate in terms of coverage and timing?*

Coverage and timing are important not only in terms of the target audience and their purchasing characteristics and behaviour, but also from the point of view of integration with the other elements of the marketing mix, notably sales and distribution. It is a fundamental theorem of marketing that demand-stimulation through advertising must be coordinated with the means of demand satisfaction, i.e. enough stock in enough outlets. Yet even today in company after company, we find this process of synchronization is not achieved, largely because of unrealistic assumptions about production availability, physical distribution capability, sales force ability to sell-in and merchandising ability to achieve display. Mass advertising is only justified where mass demand can be created and satisfied by mass distribution; this relationship needs careful and regular checking.

3   *Is the agency fully briefed on the markt situation and company activities and is it managed effectively?*

The case history raised many questions about the client/agency relationship. Undoubtedly some of the problems arose because the agency was insufficiently briefed, some because the agency's work had not been thoroughly scrutinized. The role and function of the agency need to be clearly defined if both client and agency are to achieve jointly the best results.

The evaluation of advertising effectiveness continues to tax the minds of clients and agencies alike. Much research has been conducted into advertising sales relationships and some useful conclusions can be drawn, for example that in some consumer goods markets, those companies wishing to maintain a given market share need to spend more than that percentage of the total advertising in the market. Interestingly, despite the considerable efforts made to achieve creative approaches, the creative impact is normally ignored by the analysts who attempt to demonstrate relationships simply between results (sales, share, etc.) and expenditure!

While recognizing the value of much of the research, it is our opinion that the real problem of assessing advertising stems from the lack of a complete concept, in most companies, of its role and function within the total promotional mix. A communications model allied to a model of the total market mechanism at least offers a systematic approach. This does imply considerable research, if it is to be quantified and not simply used as a framework. However, any research spending should be weighed against the often vast amounts of money spent on advertising itself. Although most managements seem unhappy with the old epigram that 50 per cent of their expenditure is wasted, oddly they seem unwilling to spend even 5 per cent on research to attempt to identify the ineffective half.

Sales promotion

This is normally defined by exclusion; it usually embraces all promotional activities not included in PR, advertising or personal selling. The methods are legion – competitions, special offers, sampling, demonstration, displays, merchandise award schemes, exhibitions, direct marketing etc. However, using the market system model, it is possible to subdivide these activities into three categories: promotions to the trade, promotions to the consumer or end-user and promotions at the interface of trade and consumer or end-user. The great advantage of sales promotion techniques is that beause they are specific and normally short-term, it is possible to identify in each of the categories specific objectives and thus evaluate the relevance and the effectiveness of the methods employed. Generally sales promotion is best used to overcome particular problems or exploit special opportunities within the context of the demand pull (created by advertising) and the product push (driven by the sales force).

It is in this latter area that the first category of promotions to the trade applies. There may be particular problems in the general selling-in process of persuading distributors to take stock of a new product or to stock up on established lines before a new advertising campaign. The sales force's task can be eased by sales promotions, such as dealer loaders, special offers, special discount or rebate schemes etc. Because of the specificity of the situation, very clear goals can and should be set, such as increasing stocks in distributors from two to three week's supply, to encourage a given number of new outlets to stock the product, to gain particular displays, etc.

Likewise, in the demand pull activity, there may be particular objectives for which advertising is too general an approach. To move consumers from conviction of the benefits of the product to the point of trial can often be helped by sampling or use of coupons on a local or more widespread basis. Likewise consumer competitions can encourage involvement and repeat purchasing in a more specific way than can media advertising. Again it is possible to set quantitative goals for such activities.

Having sold the product into the distributive outlets and persuaded the consumers who visit the outlets to at least try and, it is hoped, repeatedly buy it, the manufacturer must ensure that the shopper can readily find the product and be further motivated to purchase it rather than the competitive offerings. The third category of sales promotions which take place at this interface is normally termed merchandising and includes all the techniques of in-store positioning, shelf and special displays, signing, demonstration and sampling etc. Once again, the promotional task is specific – to ensure that it is made as easy as possible for consumers to find, to be finally convinced and to purchase the product.

Given this background, it is therefore the task of the marketing auditor to assess the following.

1   *Have all the 'pressure points' been identified in the total marketing system where there are particular problems and/or opportunities, where the general sales and advertising activity needs support?*

Although sales promotion is most widely used by consumer goods companies selling through distributive channels, there are numerous opportunities in other industries. For example, an office equipment company found that although its sales force was effective when face to face with the customer, the real difficulty was getting in front of enough potential purchasers particularly of the right level. They needed additional motivation to encourage them to spare the time to inspect the equipment and discuss it with the salesmen. The company therefore purchased an old sailing barge and equipped it as a floating demonstration centre. Potential buyers found visiting this unusual boat a much more attractive proposition than the normal routine of seeing a salesman at the office or visiting an ordinary showroom. Likewise, agricultural machinery manufacturers have long recognized that sceptical farmers will be more convinced by competitive trials than any amount of glossy advertising although that can play a significant role in creating brand awareness.

2   *Have the specific promotional goals been set and appropriate techniques employed to achieve those goals?*

Too often the novelty or creativity of the promotional idea or even its apparent low cost can distract management from the objectives of the exercise and the need to use relevant promotional methods. In one extreme case, an agricultural chemical manufacturer developed a sophisticated but expensive garden product which it decided to launch, using, among other techniques, money-off coupons to encourage sampling, a well proven (albeit costly) method. However, they were offered and accepted a financially attractive proposition to place the coupons in a free advertising newspaper which was distributed direct to many thousands of homes. The promotion was a complete disaster, only a handful of coupons being redeemed and some of those from outlets which did not even stock the product! Hindsight revealed that not only was the paper inappropriate in image for their sophisticated, expensive product, consisting as it did of large numbers of advertisements for army surplus equipment, rupture appliances etc., but also the reason for its cheapness was that distribution costs were saved by concentrating on apartment blocks. Thus, although the circulation was certainly very large, it was mainly to households without gardens, an insuperable barrier when trying to sell a garden product!

3   *Is each promotion carefully evaluated in terms of its contribution to the total promotional objectives?*

Too often promotions are evaluated simply on their own terms. Thus the effectiveness of a cut-price merchandising display for two weeks in a store is measured by the sales in that fortnight. This tells the Marketing Director very little. It is well accepted that if price is cut, sales will increase, but often to a level that at best only recoups the costs of the promotion. The only valid reason for promoting in this way is to encourage wider sampling followed by continued purchasing. Thus the assessment of the effectiveness of the promotion should be based on the running rate of sale before and after it takes place. In many cases, all the promotion has achieved is the pulling forward of sales that would have been made anyway.

An analogous situation for the industrial manufacturer is the use of exhibitions where, again all too often, although many people might visit the stand, thus making it appear successful, more thorough analysis shows that adequate contact was already being maintained with most of them. This is not an argument against the use of exhibitions, but one for more precision in the definition of their goals in the context of the total promotional objectives of the firm.

Personal selling

The personal sales activity is primarily concerned with persuasion at the first level of contact between the manufacturer and his market. For those companies selling through distributive channels, the sales activity will be directed at wholesalers, retailers, distributors, dealers etc. For those selling direct it will be aimed at customers such as other manufacturers (e.g. capital equipment) other businesses (e.g. office equipment), specifiers (e.g. doctors for pharmaceuticals, architects for building supplies) or domestic consumers (e.g. door-to-door selling). In most cases, but certainly not all (e.g. pharmaceuticals), orders are taken by or can be attributed to the salesman, thus allowing an assessment of performance. In auditing sales activities, however, a fuller analysis of the role and function should be undertaken along the lines of the following questions.

1   *What is the nature of the sales task and how is it changing?*
Chapter 1 discussed the changes occurring in the marketplace, distributive

systems and technology, particularly computerization. All these factors are affecting the traditional role of the salesman and it is advisable therefore to reconsider what it is the personal sales activity is supposed to do. This reassessment should start by reviewing what the salesman can and should do to persuade today's customer to buy. Data for such a customer service requirements analysis may be drawn from the perception surveys described earlier.

From such a study in one packaging company it was shown that whereas traditionally the customer had wanted information on product specification, prices, delivery etc., today, because of increased competition in the customer's own market, he needed help on the use of packaging design as a marketing tool. In another case we demonstrated that oil and lubricants distributors needed help with developing their own local marketing activities, not simply persuasion about how much they should buy of what products.

In general, there is a strong trend in all sales jobs whereby the emphasis is changing from the 'selling-in' aspects to the 'selling-out' features. This is making the sales task more complex, a complexity which is further enhanced by the increasingly specific characteristics and requirements of different customer groups. For example, big customers need very different servicing from small customers, not simply because of the scale of their business but because the nature of their business is different. Typically the large customer increasingly demands product modification (even to the level of having its own brands as in the food trade), individual promotional support, special prices, credit terms, delivery arrangements etc., all on national and ever more frequently an international scale. At the same time, small customers are tending to become more specialized and more expensive to service.

2 *How can these changing customer requirements be satisfied?*
Traditionally all the servicing requirements of the customers in an area were fulfilled by the territory salesman. Because of the changing nature of the sales task, increasingly this is neither possible nor economic. The range of skills and responsibilities is now often beyond the scope of one individual, encompassing financial negotiation, marketing analysis, promotional experience, knowledge of computer systems etc., as well as the traditional sales function. Many companies have concluded that some of the field sales tasks, for example routine re-ordering, can be handled by other means such as telephone selling, van selling, and increasingly on-line computer systems, thus releasing sales force time for the more complex tasks, for instance high level negotiation. In examining these tasks, many organizations have decided that one person cannot efficiently handle all types of customers and have restructured their field forces so that particular teams of salesmen can concentrate on groups of similar customers. The organizational implications of this are explored further in Chapter 7.

The auditor of a current field sales operation will need to satisfy himself that appropriate cost-effective mechanisms are being deployed to satisfy the whole changing spectrum of customer requirements, that those requirements have been grouped appropriately in terms of their nature and that the structure of the sales activity reflects those decisions.

For example, in an industrial company operating a typical system of each salesman handling all customers in his territory, we identified basic customer service requirement differences between selling to original equipment manufacturers and to the replacement market and particularly the changing balance of importance between the two as original equipment markets became saturated, highly competitive and unprofitable. In order to recognize the difference, and to place much greater emphasis on the replacement segment, the sales force was divided into two. In the original equipment sector, the work demanded not only direct sales and negotiation skills, but engineering and production knowledge in order to persuade the customer to incorporate the component in his machinery. The replacement market, because it consisted of large numbers of small customers, was best handled through distributive networks. This demanded of the sales force not only the ability to sell the product into the distributors (some of which could be handled by teleselling), but also knowledge of the total distributive operation (i.e. warehousing, financing and marketing) in order to help the distributor to sell out to the replacement customers.

Similar analysis of consumer goods and other companies has led to the separate handling of major customers (i.e. supermarket chains) on national and regional bases, the introduction of telephone selling for routine ordering, the hiring of commando sales forces for rapid new product launching, the use of brokers to handle products which cannot support an employed sales force, and the employment of franchising to gain entrepreneurial drive behind development.

3   *Does the existing sales force have the appropriate knowledge and skills for these changing tasks?*
Obviously the knowledge and skill requirements of the sales force change with the readjustment of their role to the increasingly complex market and distributive environment. The modern salesman in most industries needs to be familiar with all the major marketing tasks (e.g. market research, product management, pricing, distribution, advertising, sales promotion), particularly where he is handling major distributive customers. In addition he usually needs a good knowledge of finance and negotiation, and often an understanding of production, computer systems, and physical distribution, all in addition to an increasingly complex product knowledge and sophisticated sales skills.

These requirements can change the recruitment profile and certainly the training needed. Training needs analysis will reveal in most companies a discrepancy between the knowledge and skills required to service the market today, and the existing expertise of the sales force. We have developed and run many hundreds of programmes to fill these gaps, covering such areas as the financial basis for negotiation in the steel products industry, distributor marketing planning for petroleum company salesmen, the use of market research data in selling packaging and merchandising techniques for automotive parts.

In some cases the auditor might conclude that today's recruitment profile is so different from that of the existing sales force that the only solution is gradually to change some or all of its members. While never an easy decision, it is one that is much better taken early than late so that natural wastage can be replaced with better suited personnel, rather than having an expensive and painful redundancy exercise.

Checking the total mix

Having examined each of the major promotional categories in some detail to assess their current individual effectiveness, the Marketing Director might again usefully reflect on the mix as a whole.

1 *Is promotional influence being brought to bear on all the key links in the total marketing chain from manufacturer to consumer or end-user?*
In companies marketing through distribution channels, we have often seen that the weakest link is in-store, where unless the product is available, visible and well presented, the total promotional effort will be jeopardized. This indicates that particular attention should be paid to merchandising in self-service outlets and to staff motivation and training where there are sales assistants. In companies marketing direct (e.g. many industrial firms, office equipment) a common weakness is an over-reliance on the direct sales effort to the buyer, thus causing underrating of other promotional techniques which can have impact on purchasers or purchasing influencers. For example, PR can often play a much larger role in industrial marketing than is commonly recognized because it can communicate cost-effectively with some of the influences that surround the industrial purchasing decision. It is a cliché of selling that the right MAN must be persuaded, MAN being a mnemonic for the person controlling the Money, the purchasing Authority and the Need. In industrial selling these three characteristics may be represented, of course, by more than one and often several different people. In evaluating the balance of the promotional mix, the Marketing Director should ensure that the relevant people are identified and communicated with; whereas often the salesman only relates regularly with the immediate buyer or buyers. For example, in selling computers, he will deal normally with the Data Processing Manager and/or Finance Director. Computer purchase decisions, because of their magnitude and corporate implications, are often taken at Board level involving Production, Marketing, R and D, Personnel Directors etc. as well as the Chairman and the Managing Director, each of whom will have an opinion and usually a vote. A total promotion mix must seek to reach all the influences but not necessarily by personal selling alone as it is an expensive medium. Thus an appropriate mix might be direct selling to the immediate purchasers backed by PR, advertising or promotion activity (e.g. relevant exhibitions) to the other buying influences. Yet in our experience few computer manufacturers seek to communicate with Marketing Directors through any medium.

2   *Are all the elements of the promotional mix congruent with each other,
    integrated and synchronized?*

If the maximum benefit is to be gained from the promotional expenditure,
the various elements of the mix should reinforce each other and present a
consistent, continuous message to the target audience which is then fulfilled
by the product. This is what Levitt has called 'centripetal marketing' and
involves not only the major categories of PR, advertising, sales promotion
and personal selling, but also the total corporate presentation of the firm –
letterheads, premises, vehicles, packaging, brochures, and those personnel
in contact with the company's 'publics'. This is particularly important in
service industries where this total corporate communication is part of the
'product'. There is little point, for example, in producing effective
advertisements convincing the market that bank managers are in reality
friendly, understanding, expert and accessible if the customer who attempts
to see one is impeded by unhelpful counter clerks before eventually meeting
a manager who has not been adequately briefed or trained in what he
perceives resentfully as a debasement of his traditional role. Similar
examples of lack of congruence between advertisements, brochures, staff
response, etc. and the services provided spring to mind from the package
holiday industry, airline marketing and many of the public utilities and
services.

Product marketing can also suffer from lack of congruence, integration
and particularly synchronization. It is commonplace to find, for example,
the complete historical range of corporate logos covering the last 20 years
still displayed on various dealer premises despite huge effort and cost
expended by manufacturers on new housestyles and advertising. Firms
proudly proclaim their worldwide capability, but lack brochures in any
language other than their own; organizations urge potential customers to
contact them and leave them hanging on at the switchboard before telling
them that the department concerned does not seem to be answering its
telephones at the moment; or most wasteful of all, those companies which
promote demand for their product successfully, but then fail to make it
available to the expectant market.

3   *Are all reasonable efforts being made to evaluate the cost-effectiveness of
    the elements of the promotional mix individually and in total?*

It is a curious fact that marketing management seems much more motivated
to plan and implement promotional activity than to evaluate its success.
Money spent on research or experimentation in order to assess effectiveness
is often seen as a waste of good money that could have been spent on even
more promotion, although there is no certainty that the promotion monies
themselves are well spent. It has been argued that this attitude springs from
advertising agencies who might be perceived as having a vested interest in
not discovering whether 50 per cent is wasted. However true this may be, it
seems unlikely to be the only reason, because the attitude is found in areas
of promotion other than those in which agencies are involved, e.g. personal
selling. Whatever the cause, the effect tends to be that insufficient effort is
put into the evaluation of results and thus justification of action. This can be

readily demonstrated by questions such as: Is the PR expenditure cost-effective? Why is the advertising appropriation the level that it is? Why are there the number of salesmen that there are? etc.

The fact that evaluation is difficult and imperfect should not stop the Marketing Director pressing for assessment. This means, as was suggested at the beginning of this section, the development of some hypotheses about how promotion works and continuous effort to validate and improve them – two concepts have been indicated which could prove helpful. One thing is certain – unless a company tries to measure the effectiveness of its past promotional activity, it has no solid basis for planning future action.

Broader implications of the marketing audit

The marketing audit is designed to evaluate how effectively and competitively the marketing activity (products, prices, distribution and promotion) is satisfying the ever changing needs of the various components – consumers, distributors, customers – of the market system. These two chapters have focused on some of the key directorial and managerial aspects of the audit rather than the detailed techniques, because it is our experience that it is often the basic premises upon which the marketing activity is founded that really need review, rather than the sophisticated veneer of marketing tactics. Of course, it is important to consider in detail whether one advertising medium is more cost-effective per thousand than another, what colour the packaging should be or how the after-sales service can be better organized. We find, however, that such considerations can distract top management from the more fundamental issues such as whether the product is so competitively unsatisfying to the market that even the best advertising, packaging and after-sales service can make only a marginal difference and what is really required is a complete redesign or replacement. One of the significant contributions regular auditing can make is to identify such issues early enough for top management to take the appropriate action; auditing should not be left until severe problems arise because by then the only possible short-term solution is usually to intensify promotional activity. The true marketing concept of assessing market needs and producing satisfactions to meet them can only operate on a lengthy time-scale in most industries. The difficult balance that the company must achieve is selling effectively what is currently made in the short term, while identifying and developing what can be sold in the long term. In a rapidly evolving world these two processes are becoming increasingly difficult.

This focus on basic issues is important, not only because of the changing environment, but also because it is all too easy for top senior management perception and attitudes to become unduly influenced by their own particular past experiences (rapidly outdated) or by the partial and sometimes biased information provided by subordinates. It can be very difficult for the Marketing Director, particularly in a company of any size operating internationally, to keep in touch personally with all the realities of the marketplace. He must, of course, rely on his judgement and his staff, but it is wise to check these regularly by some form of audit process. It will have been noted that emphasis has been laid on the need for objectively researched data throughout the discussion of the marketing audit; this is because it has been our repeated experience that management attitudes often do not match the realities of the current conditions of operation.

In one paper packaging manufacturer, for example, the whole management team believed that the most important factor in selling was the speed with which enquiries were followed by quotations. Therefore considerable resources had been deployed in the estimating department and we were informed with pride that their quotations always arrived before the competitors'. Research with the customers revealed, however, that the buyers were not so impressed because at that stage of the buying process they had to wait for all the competitive quotations to be submitted before they could make their purchasing decisions. Moreover the first company to quote was often at a disadvantage because a skilful competitive salesman could discover what the quotation contained and position his own accordingly. The buyer's main concern was to receive samples as quickly as possible as these were needed for production and marketing evaluation, and this aspect of our client's service was heavily criticized, particularly as it did not match the speed and efficiency of their estimating. This was largely because the management had not recognized its importance. Why management had developed attitudes to estimating and sample making which were exactly the reverse of those held by buyers they were trying to serve, we never discovered. It might have been an over-reaction to the opinions of a few vociferous buyers who in the past had needed quick quotations. It may have been a gradual evolution in the pattern of purchasing behaviour. Whatever the reasons, it is not an isolated case. We regularly discover companies who believe their products are bought because of their high technical quality, although competitive offerings are seen as equally good by buyers who are actually much more concerned about availability, delivery, service or credit terms.

As well as emphasis on collecting objective data, stress has been laid on the need to develop deeper understanding of how the total marketing system works. The process of marketing can be defined as the management of cause-effect relationships. The company decides the effects it wants to produce – sales, profit, market share – and then tries to influence the causes that will produce those effects – consumer, distributor, customer purchasing behaviour. The means of influence are, of course, products, prices, distribution activity and promotion. However, deciding how to influence, and by how much, to produce the desired effects involves knowing, albeit imperfectly, how the whole set of causal relationships works.

Such concepts, of course, exist in any company that continues to stay in business, but often there seems insufficient effort made to refine and update the understanding of the market mechanism, particularly in overseas markets which may work very differently. Even simple modelling, as has been suggested, can make a significant contribution to the more cost-effective direction of marketing activity, even though early models may have to be crude and insufficiently quantified. Moreover, they provide a framework into which new data and experiences can be fitted and against which current activities can be appraised. For example, a joint study by A. C. Nielsen,* the research agency, and Leo Burnett, an international advertising agency, into the characteristics of leading brands in 25 consumer goods markets provides a number of conclusions which most Marketing Directors will find thought-provoking. This research showed that the brand leaders in these markets maintained prices 7 per cent above the market average, that their share of the total advertising in their markets was 5 per cent more than their market share, that despite this their advertising cost to sales revenue ratio at 6 per cent was lower than the average, that they achieved much higher levels of distribution than even their nearest competitors and, perhaps most interesting of all, that of the 25 brand leaders in 1970, 17 were still at the top in 1978. How far the conclusions of this and other similar studies can be related to different markets is a question of judgement or, preferably, further research and experimentation. Moreover, the fact that these leading brands have some common characteristics does not prove that their success is due to them. However it is only by continuous research followed by application and testing of the conclusions that our understanding of the causal relationships inherent in the marketing activity can be improved.

Auditing the various elements of the marketing activity will often raise broader questions about the present marketing objectives and strategies of the company, and the planning, organization and control of the marketing function. Indeed, one of its key purposes is to provide a total, objective and systematic review of the external opportunities and threats and the internal strengths and weaknesses of the current activity on which to base any future redirection or restructuring. Furthermore, the market audit will often reveal the need to examine other areas of company operation such as production, finance, R and D or even general management. We have found many cases, for example, where the effectiveness of the marketing activity has been seriously impaired by the inability of production to produce either to the quality standards or to the volumes required, by the lack of accurate product cost information and by the failure to provide technical development plans on time. Even where the relationships between the various functions are working smoothly, it can be worthwhile extending the marketing audit to examine how these interfaces might be made even more productive. Often minor rebalancing of the product mix, from a marketing point of view, can yield significant production savings; promotional activity to flatten a seasonal sales pattern may achieve substantial cash flow advantages; given a more specific marketing brief, R and D may find it easier to be productive and so on. Finally, if a corporate general management, for instance, fully appreciated the growing power of distributors, they might feel less inclined to chop the brand promotion budget every time they needed to find a little more profit margin!

In summary, regular, objective, systematic auditing of the marketing

---

*'What Makes a Top Brand?', *Nielsen Researcher*, no. 3, 1979.

activity in the light of the changing networks and markets and *vis-à-vis* competition is a powerful method by which the Marketing Director can assess its current effectiveness, identify its relationships with the other activities of the company, and develop a better understanding of the whole mechanism of causal relationships. Furthermore, it provides a sound basis for considering the company's future direction and how the corporate objectives can best be achieved.

CHECKLIST

1 *Public relations*

1.1 With which target audiences should we be communicating?
1.2 What are their levels of knowledge, attitude and opinion about the company?
1.3 What do we want them to think and feel about the company?
1.4 Do we check to see whether the PR activity has caused the desired changes in knowlege, attitude and opinion?

2 *Advertising*

2.1 Are the target audiences specified clearly?
2.2 Are our messages likely to be persuasive?
2.3 Is the agency properly briefed and controlled?
2.4 Is the advertising measured against the communication objectives set for it?

3 *Sales promotion*

3.1 Have 'pressure points' been identified where sales promotion can be used effectively?
3.2 Have specific promotion goals been set?
3.3 Do the techniques selected match the goals?
3.4 Are the promotions evaluated in terms of the overall mix objectives?

4 *Personal selling*

4.1 How is the nature of the sales task changing?
4.2 Should other methods of contacting the customer (e.g. teleselling, van selling) be considered?
4.3 Does the existing sales force have the appropriate knowledge and skill?
4.4 Is the sales force appropriately structured and staffed?

5 *Checking the total mix*

5.1 Does the total promotional activity cover every element in the market system?
5.2 Are the elements of the promotional mix congruent, integrated and synchronized?
5.3 Is sufficient time, effort and money being spent on evaluation of the effectiveness of the mix in total and of each element?
5.4 Do we have a solid basis for planning future promotional action?

6 *Broader implications of the marketing audit*

6.1 Are we auditing early and regularly enough to allow adequate consideration of the key issues, not simply the current problems?

6.2 Do we know how accurately current management perceptions, attitudes and opinions reflect present realities?

6.3 Are we improving our concepts and models of the market mechanism and its workings?

6.4 Is the marketing activity inhibited by or inhibiting the effectiveness of the other functions of the organization?

Part II

WHERE DO WE WANT TO GO?

Chapter 5

Deciding the Corporate Marketing Direction

A prime function of every top management team is the setting of objectives specifying what the organization is to achieve in the future and in broad terms how it will go about achieving them. Any organization above the survival level always has a number of alternative directions from which it can select and a choice of routes to each destination. However, because of scarcity of resources and competitive pressure, not all directions can be followed simultaneously because such a policy not only means achieving little in any direction, but also tends to lead the company into a vicious spiral as the management and staff, feeling lost and leaderless, wander round in ever-decreasing circles.

The need for objectives and strategies can hardly be doubted if the company wishes to prosper; but particularly today, top management of which of course the Marketing Director is a key member, seem to find it difficult to define what kind of objectives are needed, how they can be derived, what criteria should be set, how often they should be reviewed and most important of all, how they can be applied in the running of the business. Often insufficient time is devoted to longer-term considerations because of the pressures of short-term problems and opportunities. It can be difficult for the top management team involved to stand back far enough to achieve a true perspective on the business, and there is often an underlying suspicion that even if objectives were constructed they would be of little practical help.

The last point is certainly true of many statements of objectives we see, such as 'we intend making as much money as possible every year', 'we are in the communications (or energy, or leisure, or any other buzz-word) business', 'we aim to be the best in the industry'. They may sound trendy, virtuous or commercially tough, but they contribute little to deciding the corporate future.

Setting corporate marketing objectives

For the purposeful direction of the corporate marketing activity, objectives should be derived from answering the following questions:

1 What business are we in?
2 What profits do we want to make?
3 How fast do we want to grow?

What business are we in?

No apology is made for returning to a question that has been discussed for so long that it is part of marketing folklore, and is familiar to any first-year student at business school. Perhaps it is because it has been around so long that the practical analysis of its meaning seems not to have progressed. Virtually every Marketing Director and most of his top management colleagues accept the basic concepts of the business as a consumer-identifying and satisfying organization, and seen through the customer's eyes, of the business perceived in terms of the needs it satisfies, rather than the products it happens to be making.

Most executives are familiar with statements that if only the railways had seen themselves in the transport industry or Hollywood in the entertainment business, rather than as film-makers, they might have avoided some of the problems that befell them. Such concepts, while possessing an essential truth, need to be refined much more if they are to be of practical use in the operation of the company. Furthermore, they ignore the history, the resources, the reputation and the management capabilities that are particular to any firm. Thus, to refine the example given above, Hollywood's real mistake was not its failure to see itself in entertainment, but to underrate the changing pattern of distribution in the entertainment market. TV was not so much a competitor as a more convenient means of distributing entertainment; once that had been realized, it opened up significant marketing possibilities, not only for making special TV films, but also for those film companies with large libraries to exploit an under-utilized resource by renting or selling old movies, first to the TV companies and subsequently on videotape to the domestic market.

Thus to answer the question 'what business are we in?' involves understanding not only the changing consumer needs to be satisfied, but also the evolution of the whole market mechanism in the light of the company's own history and resources. Then the question can often be answered in a way which defines practical objectives which can be implemented.

For example, working with a scaffolding company, we helped them reach a specification of the business which certainly created particular opportunities which they have since profitably exploited. The first raising of the question 'what business are we in?' caused the normal reaction of most management teams – boredom and irritation at re-examining a question which had yielded no results in the past and to which the answer was surely self-evident: 'scaffolding for the building industry'. This is usually the nature of the first answer which merely defines the current product offering to the current (and usually historic) market.

The second stage was to analyse what other markets had needs that could be satisfied by scaffolding. The original answer was the 'building industry', because this had been a growth market in the early '70s, especially in south-east England where the company was located, and all attention had been directed to it. However, analysis quickly showed that other industries (e.g. chemical plant) need scaffolding; broadening the managerial view to 'the construction industry' led to the search for new opportunities especially as the building industry was declining. Far away from the company head office, in the north-east of Scotland, the offshore oil and gas industry was expanding, requiring more oil rigs, on-shore installations, etc., all in an area which had been so low in 'building' potential that the company had not even had a salesman there. With virtually no change needed in the product, the firm was able to develop a significant and growing business once the potential had been identified.

The third stage was to examine the product more closely to identify its essence, i.e. what it did rather than what it was. Discussion with the management team produced the definition that it gave 'temporary access and support' thus leading to a search for other needs that could be satisfied by such benefits. One aspect of the leisure industry is the development of events such as shows and sporting fixtures (e.g. mayoral processions, horse trials, golf tournaments, pop concerts) into major spectacles requiring seating accommodation. Scaffolding, by its nature, can be used to construct such temporary grandstands.

The fourth stage was to examine that essence and to identify the competitive abilities of the company in providing it. In other words, all scaffolding firms can provide 'temporary access and support' for the building, construction or leisure industries; what was particular about the way this company provides it? After long complex arguments about the relative advantage of different types of jointing system, it was eventually concluded that although technical differences did exist, all the competitive systems satisfied about equally the same need of holding the tubes together.

Further analysis of the nature of the business showed, however, that the company's success had been founded on the speed and safety with which they erected and dismantled the scaffolding. Most scaffolding is bought or rented on the basis of competitive quotation or tender. Costs are very similar between competing companies because they draw their tube and other supplies from the same sources and the labour force tends to be paid on the same industry-wide basis. Thus it is difficult either to raise prices or to lower prime cost in order to increase profitability. Profit differences could be and had been made by our client by developing more efficient methods of erection and dismantling followed by intensive training of the personnel involved. This expertise was the major differentiating factor and its recognition caused further opportunities to be received.

The company had never seriously considered overseas markets because scaffolding tube, the basic element of the product, is very costly to ship, and in any case is available in most countries for their own indigenous scaffolding industries. However, expertise can be exported. An investigation of the suddenly rich Middle Eastern markets soon showed that the tremendous construction boom of hotels, hospitals, refineries, etc., was causing many scaffolding problems. In most countries there had been little high-rise construction before the oil dollars were available to finance the ambitious building programmes and little local expertise was to be had in scaffolding these types of construction, resulting in the use of slow and often unsafe methods. Our client therefore planned to open training schools for scaffolding supervisors and operatives in a number of Middle Eastern centres and thus profit from his skills by charging fees for attendance.

This case history has been presented at length because it demonstrates how even a company with, on the face of it, a relatively simple product/ market situation can benefit from a considered response to the question 'what business are we in?' It is a question that can only be answered when top management, guided by the Marketing Director, understand the full range of changing needs to be satisfied at all levels in the market system, perceive the real essence of the products or services they do or could supply, and objectively identify the uniqueness (or at least the competitive advantage) of the company and how it can be exploited. Regular marketing audits, of course, provide much of the information that is needed to assess the current strengths and weaknesses, and thus help identify future opportunities and constraints.

What profits do we want to make?

The role and definition of financial objectives seems to cause some confusion in many organizations. In a commercial enterprise is profit the only true end to which everything else, like marketing objectives, are simply the means? Or, is it not an objective at all, but a resource and a yardstick by which progress towards other objectives, social as well as commercial, can be financed and measured?

Without wishing to enter the philosophical or sociological debates, the role and definition of profit objectives is central to the decisions on corporate direction and therefore must be considered.

Making profits is obviously essential to the survival of any commercial enterprise; otherwise it cannot finance its own continuance at its current levels (the requirement of security), it cannot plan to expand (the requirement of growth), and it cannot service its capital whether provided by shareholders, banks, government or private owners (the requirement of yield). Insufficient profits therefore cause stagnation, and more often decline, leading to lower employment, lower individual and corporate tax to finance other investments or social programmes, etc. It is thus relatively simple to see why profits are necessary and what level they need to reach to satisfy security, growth and yield criteria. The practical problem is to decide how far above that minimum level the objective should be set.

This will depend partially on the kind of business the company is in, and that is why the objective must be settled first. Different industries at different times vary in profitability, and although individual firms can achieve very different results within the same industry, nevertheless the nature of the business does, to a degree, determine its potential profitability.* The history and structure of the firm will also affect the future profit possibilities at least in the short-term run of, say, two to three years. If it has made recent heavy investments in plant and machinery (e.g. chemicals) the profitability may be limited by the market's ability to absorb the additional output quickly.

Finally, and most important of all, how far above the minimum the company should go will be determined by management's judgement about what is realistic, albeit challenging, without jeopardizing the other goals of the company, notably the longer-term development of markets, products and the people within the business. Actions such as reducing advertising, stopping product development, freezing staff levels and pay, will all in the short term increase profits but, as any experienced manager knows, at the serious risk of damaging the longer term.

The alternative approach to setting profit objectives is to treat them as the only true goals and move from business to business as one appears more profitable than the other. However, such 'City whizz-kid' approaches do not seem to be very successful, judging by the recent history of such financially oriented conglomerates. Simple profit criteria may be valid for the investor, but are of limited help to the business manager.

Setting profit objectives is difficult because they can only be calculated as minima, because the achievement of maximum short-term levels can destroy the future and of themselves objectives give no indication of what the business should be doing. It is not surprising, therefore, that regardless of what management teams may say about 'profit being the name of the game' and 'our job is to maximize profits', most successful companies set realistic profit objectives (obviously above the minimum, but certainly below the short-term maximum), and use them as criteria for judging both performance and potential developments. In running the business, however, they usually find other types of objective, such as marketing goals, much more helpful. One study showed that companies who set profit objectives in this way tend to be more profitable than firms who simply try to make as much money as possible.†

---

*A *Financial Times* analysis of 620 companies spanning 27 industry categories showed a range of profitability from 38 per cent in the most profitable industry to 8.5 per cent in the least profitable in 1978/79. ('Trend of Industrial Profits', *Financial Times*, 29 October 1979). †'Management Policies and Practices and Business Performance', Centre for Interfirm Comparison, 1977.

Profit objectives are therefore an extremely useful form of goal, particularly when amplified via the mechanism of 'return on capital employed', and its supporting ratios. They represent both ends to be achieved and criteria for measuring progress towards those ends. They provide a basis for comparing alternative courses of action, and the means to achieving them. But profit objectives of themselves do not help define the future nature and direction of the business which is absolutely necessary if management is to plan where the company should be going and how it will get there.

How fast do we want to grow?

Most companies seem to want some statement of growth embodied in their objectives. This is usually because it is felt that if the company does not grow it will stagnate or fall behind; this is patently true in terms of market position if the market is growing. Furthermore, in public companies, there is often a strong and reasonable feeling that the shareholders want to see their investment and earnings grow. Also management itself enjoys the prestige of growth and recognizes that it is much easier to recruit and retain good people in a so-called 'growth company'. However, the concept of growth is seldom defined with any precision, perhaps because for so many years it could be simply equated with growth in volume, leading to growth in size, staff and profits. If profits need to grow to fund expansion or satisfy shareholders, this does not necessarily mean volume growth in the existing business; perhaps it would be wiser to eliminate unproductive costs or to diversify. If it is felt that the management and staff need to feel 'growth', this may be better provided by additional challenges such as tackling more complex job opportunities, different markets, greater responsibilities. Even where markets are growing, there may be an optimum level of market share beyond which the effort, risk and cost more than offset the benefits of volume sales gain.

This is not to deny growth as a valid objective, but to attempt to define what it should mean and to suggest that in particular circumstances there may be an optimum level of share, staffing and even volume and profits, expansion beyond which creates more risk and potentially lower perform-ance. For example, a large chartered accountancy practice has had to develop an optimum volume growth objective based on the responsibilities and rewards of the partners who are both a major resource and the top management team. If it expands more slowly than this growth level, it will inevitably cause crowding and demotivation throughout the staff hierarchy as there will be too many senior executives amongst whom to divide the responsibilities of partnership; if it expands faster there will be too few qualified and experienced managers at any level to maintain the high quality and amount of work which is the essence of their business.

Optimum share levels and growth are specified in some companies which recognize that beyond such levels, competitive or governmental attention may become vastly intensified. Even too rapid growth in profits may not only attract new competitors but also raise shareholders' expectations to a level that cannot be maintained, particularly if profit growth is achieved at the expense of future investment.

Translating marketing objectives into operating goals

The setting of corporate marketing objectives starts with a thorough analysis of the implications of the question 'what business are we in?'. This should result in at least a 'mission statement' defining the business from the marketplace inwards; usually it gives more precise answers in terms of markets to be served and the essential nature, benefits and competitive advantage of the corporate offering. From this a statement of desired market profile should be constructed. Thus, one company in the security industry redefined its desired profile as 'a major, technologically advanced, competent and responsible supplier of fire, property and personal protection'. They then specified what each of the words meant, e.g. 'major' meant in the top three suppliers in each selected market segment holding a minimum 25 per cent share. The objective could therefore be used as a basis for more specific target setting, not only in terms of sales and share, but also to set communication goals for the promotional activity. How far the target audiences perceived the company as having this profile is thus measurable before and after any PR or advertising activity.

The definition of profit objectives should include not only absolute amounts, but also their relationship with capital employed and sales broken down as far as possible in terms of volume, price, mix, cost and asset utilization targets so that practical criteria are available for appraising performance and intended developments.

Growth objectives should recognize the many different forms of growth other than simple increases in sales volume, and also the point that growth may not be possible, or desirable beyond an optimum level. This may stimulate the company to search for other separate business opportunities where they are not so constrained.

All the objectives set should be checked to ensure they are specific, where possible quantified, and given a time-scale. There is little point setting objectives unless performance can be measured against them and the degree of achievement evaluated. Care needs to be taken in their specification, as in the security company case above, so that even each word is given as precise a definition as possible. An excellent way of checking the utility of an objective is to consider how performance will be assessed aganst it. This forces specificity and often quantification. Words like 'leader', 'best', 'highest quality', can and should be specified and quantified if the objective is to be of practical value. Obviously sales volume, revenue, share, mix, margin, costs and profits can all be given quantitative targets and are therefore useful criteria, but they still need to be set in a time-scale; 'long-term' simply is not good enough.

The appropriate time-scale for the objectives will depend on the nature of the business and its markets. In the light of the volatile changes in the environment, the shortest possible period ahead should be chosen and must be in line with the investment characteristics and the degree of change implied. The reason for having objectives is to give more purposeful direction to the company and its people than is inherent in the day-to-day running of the business. In a rapidly changing world the staff are likely to be as confused by the insistence on an increasingly outdated 10-year time horizon as they are by constant annual change. On average, a three to five-year ahead period for these types of objective is as long as is practicable, but thorough annual review is essential to ensure they are still valid.

The objectives should finally be assessed to ensure that the company's present or intended uniqueness or competitive advantage is embodied within them. There is little point deciding on an objective to become, in three years' time exactly similar to today's competition! Furthermore, the whole set of objectives should be reviewed to ensure that not too many have been set. We have discussed objectives here on the basis of each company only being in one business; in fact many companies are in several different businesses, or at least markets. It is tempting either to set many different objectives (all implying the use of the same resources) or to attempt an all-embracing definition which is generally useless as suggested before. To say a railway is in the transport business, while accurate, is not very helpful. The needs of people as opposed to freight, business travellers as opposed to holidaymakers, coal as opposed to automobile transport, and the competitive implications in each sector mean it is essential to consider each element almost as a separate business; moreover success in one segment may well jeopardize the achievement of objectives in another as they share to a large degree resources of track, rolling stock, money and top management time.

Most successful companies are highly selective about how much they try to achieve, recognizing that corporate commitment to relatively few key objectives is more likely to produce results than spreading the scarce resources of finance, manpower and particularly management in too many, albeit highly attractive, directions.

Selecting corporate marketing strategies

Closely related to the objective setting process is the formulation of marketing strategies. While the strategies are primarily the plans of campaign by which the objectives will be achieved, successful strategies can in turn often suggest new or redefined objectives.

Strategies are important because they provide the framework within which the tactical activities of marketing – products, prices, distribution activity, promotion – can be planned so that they head in the same direction in an integrated, synergistic way. Without a strategic overview, each element tends to be viewed separately, decisions are taken in isolation and sometimes in contradiction of each other. The questions that were raised in Chapter 4 about integrating the promotion mix are much easier to answer given clearly defined strategies.

The matrix shown in Figure 5.1 provides a useful basis for reviewing the strategic alternatives.

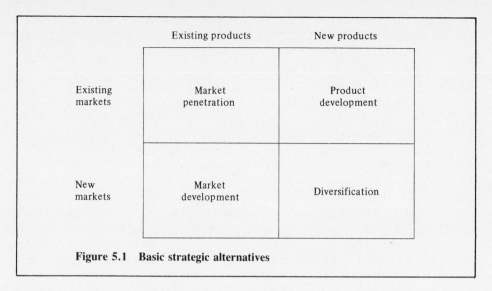

Figure 5.1   Basic strategic alternatives

Market penetration strategies

These should be considered where the market is growing or where market share is low or threatened in some or all of the markets. Such strategies normally involve clearer definition and segmentation of the market and more careful product or brand positioning. Markets such as cars, washing powder and cigarettes demonstrate such segmentation-based strategies, followed through with multiple branding in the case of washing powder, precise brand positioning (cigarettes) and a multiplicity of product variation on basic models in each segment of the car market.

The key problem of market segmentation strategy is not the definition of the segments themselves, but the selection from the available segments of those for concentration. In our experience, top management finds it easier to decide to enter new segments, rather than accept the necessary retreat from existing ones. Such decision making is helped if firm criteria are constructed against which the segments can be evaluated. Table 5.1 shows a typical list derived for a metal manufacturing company. This company was

Table 5.1

Criteria for market segment selection

(*A metal manufacturing company*)

1	Acceptable volume in relation to production capacity (quantified)
2	Adequate price levels in relation to investment and manufacturing costs (quantified)
3	Consistent growth
4	Relatively resistant to substitution by other products
5	Clear, stable distribution channels
6	Potential for significant, preferably dominant, market share

faced with capacity limitations and its objective was to market its limited output to the most attractive segments in the short and long term. Some sixteen segments were reviewed against these criteria and nine chosen for strategic and tactical concentration.

Market development strategies

These are developed from the systematic assessment of other needs that the current products or services could satisfy. They include geographic expansion as well as entry into other markets as demonstrated by the scaffolding company mentioned earlier, which moved from building into construction and leisure. One often fruitful approach is for industrial companies to examine consumer applications and vice versa. Such strategies took agricultural chemical companies into domestic garden pest and weed control, industrial adhesive firms into the DIY market, food organizations into the catering and institutional sectors and consumer electronic manufacturers into the professional user market.

The Marketing Director should, however, be cautious enough to recognize that although the needs and the product application may be apparently similar, diverse markets can work very differently. An industrial steel pipe manufacturer identified the domestic central heating market as a major opportunity, particularly as copper tube was scarce and expensive. He developed a lined steel pipe which in all tests proved perfectly satisfactory when fitted and jointed correctly so that the lining was continuous and prevented the water rusting the steel. The whole experience of the company was in selling to industry where standards of professional applications competence were tacitly accepted as a normal factor of the business. The domestic central heating market, however, particularly at the cheap end, which was the sector primarily attracted to the less costly steel pipe, is characterized by non-professional fitters, often installing central heating as a part-time activity. Their standards were such that the pipes were often not properly jointed, leakage occurred followed by rust and eventually failure of the system. Ultimately the product had to be withdrawn not because of a lack of need or its inherent features, but because the strategy had failed to recognize this critical difference in the way that market worked.

Similar problems have beset companies which, in expanding with existing products into new markets, have failed to recognize the need for different pack sizes, packaging, distribution or promotion, particularly when the new markets are overseas. One agricultural machinery manufacturer launching a new product in Germany had the embarrassing experience of discovering that the chosen model number was identical to the number of the section of the penal code dealing with homosexuality and that the number itself had become a nickname for homosexuals. Fortunately, they changed it in time thus avoiding promoting a 'gay' product to the somewhat dour farming community!

Product development

This means finding new products for existing markets, and is a valid strategic alternative where advancing technology means that the product satisfactions can be improved (e.g. electronics) or where research shows a gap between the ever-changing patterns of consumer needs and the range of product satisfactions currently offered. The growing general interest in dieting created a need in many food and beverage markets for low-calorie variations of existing products (e.g. soft drinks). Thus product development strategies can mean replacing or extending the existing range; it is obviously important to identify which, as the tactical considerations in pricing and promotion terms will be very different.

The accuracy of market segmentation is a key factor in ensuring that any new product, however novel it may seem to the company, is not perceived by the market as a simple substitute of an existing product. Some markets have become so overcrowded with products that they are more accurately described as fragmented, rather than segmented. Any new brand in the cigarette market for example has to be strategically positioned with very high accuracy if it is to stand any chance of survival without simply replacing other company products. This evolution of markets from apparently homogeneous to segmented to fragmented needs to be carefully monitored by the top marketing team as it may well mean that beyond a certain level further product development, though necessary for survival, will fail to produce significant growth. Not surprisingly, the cigarette market yields many examples of corporate diversification; because of the restrictions imposed on the total market, further product development and thus further fragmentation is unlikely to produce attractive growth for any of the participating companies.

The possibilities for product development strategies should be reviewed systematically. Can existing products be improved to increase their competitive attractiveness? Can existing products be replaced by more attractive new products? Can the existing range be extended either by modified or new products? Thus in the car market, models will be 'face-lifted' from time to time to bring them up-to-date. When market and competitive change means that even the facelifted model begins to lose its appeal, it will be replaced by a new model. At the same time the range can be extended by modification (e.g. estate car versions) or by new models, usually positioned in new and specific market segments to avoid competing with the existing range (e.g. beach buggies).

Diversification

Entering new markets with new products implies some form of diversification strategy. These alternatives usually bear the cost and risk for a company because by definition, least is known about either the market or the products that will satisfy it. The top management must therefore carefully consider their reasoning for such strategies and identify what strengths of the existing organization can be used to bridge the gap from the current to the new business. What might be termed 'negative diversification' triggered by the inability to make the present business successful is usually doomed to failure. Positive diversification seeks to capitalize on the strengths of the existing business in terms of marketing, production, technology or finance. The marketing strengths may be the corporate image which will carry from one market to another (the Cadbury name now extends from the original chocolate through to cakes and even to instant mashed potato); this depends on having an image associated with general values, for example of quality or reliability, not linked to a particular product range.

Where there are marketing strengths in distribution, the new product search may be focused on what other products the existing networks carry. Thus a component supplier enters new markets based on other products that are sold by their existing industrial distributors.

The company's success with a particular type of marketing may be used as the criterion for new market/product selection. The cigarette manufacturers have tended to diversify into businesses with similar requirements for high skill in the marketing of fast-moving consumer goods – snack foods, cosmetics, shaving requisites.

Production expertise or resources may provide a basis for entering new markets. Metal-working experience took a can manufacturer into central heating radiators; money management know-how has taken the joint stock banks into the consumer credit, unit trust and credit card markets.

Technological skills can be the common factor, thus moving an electronic calculator manufacturer into the miniaturized television business. Financial resources can take the company virtually anywhere, but unless there are other good reasons for believing that the new business can be managed effectively in terms of marketing, production, technology, etc., the simple ability to finance the development or acquisition is no guarantee that it will be successful. Conglomerates which have been assembled simply because the money was available and the acquisitions looked financially strong have still to find other synergies if they are to be continuously successful.

Two tempting directions for diversification strategies are forward and backward vertical integration. Forward integration usually involves developing, or more often, purchasing part of the distribution chain. However, unless it is perceived as a separate and different business and continued as a distributor satisfying market needs it will tend to fail. The other obvious danger is the possibility of countervailing action from other manufacturers or adverse reaction from the rest of the trade. Backward integration normally means taking control of supply facilities. Thus a machinery manufacturer who required high quality castings established his own foundry to save having to purchase them from third parties. However, for the foundry to be independently viable it had to be larger than was needed for the manufacturer's own requirements. This meant not only heavy investment, but also the development of an effective marketing activity to other castings customers. This proved particularly difficult as there was over-production in the castings industry and considerable management time and resources had to be diverted from the main machinery business to try to solve the problems of the foundry which had been originally intended to relieve the corporate top management team of the problems of purchasing castings!

Tails wagging dogs in this way are not unusual following diversification exercises. Every management team should recognize that although the grass always looks greener on the other side of the hill, the greenest grass of all usually grows on top of swamps!

Thus in the objective appraisal of alternative markets and products, management should assure itself not only that there is some synergy of marketing, production, technological or other expertise which can be utilized for successful entry, but also that it has the general creative capability and capacity to manage the new business, particularly if unforeseen problems occur at a time when there is pressure on the existing enterprise.

Evaluating and integrating the strategic approach

Although the four major categories of strategies have been discussed separately, of course combinations of two or more may provide an even more effective approach to the achievement of corporate marketing objectives. In reviewing the whole range of strategies, which is best done by starting with market penetration possibilities, followed in order by market development, product development and finally diversification potential, it will often occur that, for example, new products or methods developed to penetrate well established markets can also be used to lead the company into new markets. Whatever the strategies or combinations of strategies selected, the Marketing Director should carefully review them to check that if they are implemented successfully:

1 They will satisfy the needs of the various target groups at which they are aimed – consumers, distributors, customers, etc.
2 They will achieve the corporate marketing, financial and growth objectives.
3 They give direction to the various elements of the marketing activity – products, prices, distribution, promotion.
4 They are congruent with each other and the fulfilment of one strategy will not adversely effect the achievement of others.
5 They capitalize on the corporate strengths and minimize the effect of any weaknesses.
6 They give a competitive advantage which is difficult to match or surpass.
7 They are within the competence and resources of the company.

A good example of the successful development and implementation of integrated marketing strategy can be found in the history of a European subsidiary of a multinational food manufacturer. This company was faced with the not uncommon situation of declining growth in market consumption, rapidly reducing numbers of food outlets and the increasing dominance of big store groups, the top twenty controlling over 95 per cent of the total market. Inevitably this led to more difficulty in selling, pressure on prices, margins and thus profits, and a generally highly competitive trading situation.

The company had reacted by introducing new products through the food trade to provide more sales opportunities, strengthening the sales organization, particularly in areas such as key account management and increasing trade and consumer promotion. This constituted classic market penetration strategy which while successful in securing the short term, could not meet the longer-term profit and growth objectives of the company because of the stagnant nature of the market, the increasing pressure from the distribution network and the activities of competitors.

Further consideration suggested that the company could utilize new product development to enter new markets or at least new distribution channels. Thus a natural development from human food was into pet food which could be marketed not only through supermarkets, but also through other networks such as pet shops and butchers. This action reduced the dependence on food retailers and gave access to markets which, if not new, contained different segments as defined by different distributive networks. The original market penetration strategy was being strengthened by market development.

The expansion into new networks provided the opportunity to search for other products sold through those outlets. Pet shops, for example, sell not only pet food but also many other products for pets – dog collars, cat litter, canary bells, etc. The company diversified into such products, thus increasing the total range that could be sold to pet shops. However, these different products, as so often is the case, have quite different sales and display characteristics from the original pet food products which tend to be heavily promoted repeat purchase items. The company therefore developed new concepts of display stands and promotional support to ensure their new pet items moved through the stores. This rack merchandising approach proved to be highly successful.

The market development strategy thus led the firm into diversification with the introduction of the new pet products taking them into new markets. Furthermore an examination of their new corporate merchandising expertise led to the conclusion that it could be used as a basis for further diversification, so a search was made for other markets and products where it could be applied. This has now taken the company into the houseplant business, a totally new market served with new products through new distribution channels, a full diversification strategy.

The company's systematic and creative approach to the development of its marketing strategy has been highly successful in growth and profit terms and it is today one of the outstanding performers of the multinational group of which it is a member. It is worth noting that the process started from a difficult, static and competitive market situation where further growth and penetration were becoming increasingly hard to achieve. Product development was used as a basis for market and channel diversification, the new networks as the foundation for further new product development, the new products stimulated the evolution of new marketing and sales techniques and these in turn formed the basis for further market, distributive and product diversification. Finally it can be seen from this case not only how strategies should be developed to achieve corporate goals, but also how in turn they can cause redefinition of such objectives as 'what business are we in?' as the company added pet food, pet accessories and houseplants to its basic human food need satisfactions.

A practical approach to deciding the corporate marketing direction

Such case histories of objectives and strategy development might lead to an underestimation of the time and effort it takes to develop such approaches. The most common complaint of top management is the lack of opportunity to think about the business and where it is going. We find that even board meetings can become distracted by current crises, rather than discussing and deciding the longer-term future of the enterprise.

To overcome these problems and to create a significant opportunity for reviewing objectives and strategies, we have evolved a technique which we call 'top management workshops'. Their purpose is first to review systematically, objectively and creatively the current goals and status of the business, its problems and opportunities and its strengths and weaknesses. From that basis, the long-term objectives and strategies in the light of the changing environment and management intentions are then redefined. The workshop is attended by the whole top management team – the heads of marketing, production, finance, personnel, R and D, etc. and the General Manager, Managing Director and in some cases, Chairman. This ensures that any aspect of the business and its future can be expertly considered and decisions taken. It should be emphasized that the workshop is made realistic and effective by the actual decision making that occurs; it is not intended as a management development session, although a remarkable amount of learning usually takes place. The presence of external members, such as consultants, who are professionally experienced, is essential to ensure that traditional assumptions, attitudes and opinions are challenged and either proved or discarded. We have found that it is more effective if there are at least two external members, one of whom should take the chair; otherwise points of common agreement or familiarity tend to be tacitly accepted as true when they should be queried. It is often from the rigorous re-examination of fundamental questions that have apparently been answered satisfactorily years ago, that new initiatives are developed.

A carefully and individually constructed agenda is needed; an example is shown in Table 5.2. Discussion proceeds on the items listed, but when statements are made, they are challenged for proof. If proof is not available, such statements are set to one side for further research so that the flow is not held up. Of course, if the workshop has been preceded by a marketing audit, much of the evidence is usually to hand. Conclusions are

Table 5.2
Typical top management workshop agenda

1	Review of current corporate objectives – marketing – financial – growth
2	Review of current marketing strategies – market penetration – market development – product development – diversification
3	Analysis of opportunities, threats, strengths, weaknesses – products – pricing – distribution – advertising – promotion – sales force
4	Specification of where more information is needed (i.e. specifying research briefs)
5	Redefinition of objectives and strategies
6	Setting of action programmes

drawn at each stage, either firmly so that decisions can be taken or, where further data are required, hypotheses are constructed which can be tested. At the end of the workshop it is made clear to everybody what decisions have been reached, the tentative conclusions that need validating and the information that must be collected; it is always wise to summarize these findings in writing so that all are clear on the agreements made and the action to be taken individually.

Usually a series of workshops is needed as there is not enough time or data to reach decisions on all items. Moreover the testing of the hypotheses and the research may cause reconsideration of some of the decisions. Each workshop normally takes one day and should not take more than two days, otherwise there is a tendency to retreat into too much detail and lose the perspective which comes from maintaining the pace throughout the agenda. The intervals between workshops depend on the testing and research work to be done. Often the best solution is to hold an annual series of two, three or four before the beginning of the company planning cycle. The decisions from the last workshop can then form the framework and criteria for the marketing planning activity. We have also found that it is best to hold the workshops away from the company premises because even when interruptions are avoided (which is difficult enough), the familiar ambience of the normal place of work often stultifies creative thought and discussion.

How is a workshop different from a normal board or management planning meeting? First, it focuses entirely on the future of the company; board or management meetings often become preoccupied with, or at least are constrained by, the current results, activities and problems. Second, it involves the total top management team so that a complete review is possible and decisions can be taken; often the board does not include all functional heads and management meetings have to defer decisions for higher or wider consultation. Third, a workshop lasts much longer than the average board or management meeting so that more range and depth of discussion and thinking is possible. Fourth, the presence of external members playing a significant and professional role provides a dimension not usually found in management meetings. Even where the board has non-executive directors they may not have been appointed for their experience in objective setting and marketing strategy formulation. Fifth, most board and management meetings are held on company premises which can affect the results as suggested above.

We have had successful experience with top management workshops in fields as diverse as soft drinks, pharmaceuticals, construction services, medical equipment, aluminium rolling, domestic light fittings, professional services and government agencies. Obviously the number of workshops, the agenda, the conclusions and subsequent actions have varied. However, workshops do seem to provide an effective mechanism for deciding the corporate marketing objectives and strategies, and holding them regularly can ensure that the future direction of the firm takes account of the changing environment as well as present activities.

CHECKLIST

1   *Setting and using corporate marketing objectives*

1.1   Is there a detailed up-to-date analysis of what business(es) we are in?

1.2   Are there clear profit and profitability objectives broken down into goals for each component part of the business?

1.3   Have growth rates been defined and is there an optimum rate and/or size beyond which we should not expand?

1.4   Are the objectives practical, specific, where possible quantitative, timed, competitively advantageous and limited enough to ensure commitment?

2   *Selecting corporate marketing strategies*

2.1   Have the four major categories of strategy – market penetration, market development, product development and diversification – been investigated in turn and thoroughly?

2.2   Have the selected strategies been evaluated to ensure their relevance to the marketplace, the corporate objectives and resources, the marketing activity and the competitive situation?

2.3   Have our strategies been checked and integrated into a cohesive approach which in turn could lead to redefinition or extension of our objectives?

2.4   Do we have an effective mechanism for considering and deciding our corporate marketing direction?

Part III

HOW WILL WE GET THERE?

Chapter 6

Translating Objectives and Strategies into Marketing Plans

Most Marketing Directors find it easy to agree upon the role and importance of the marketing planning process. It is obviously essential to identify what action should be taken by whom to implement the marketing strategies and thus achieve the corporate marketing objectives and their supporting goals and targets. It is patently necessary to specify the timing and costs of these actions in order to produce programmes and budgets against which performance can be regularly reviewed. Until the marketing plan is constructed, it is difficult to produce useful plans for the other company functions, e.g. production, finance, etc. The marketing plan is not only the natural starting point for the whole corporate planning process, but also the only part of that process concerned with revenue generation. Finally, the marketing planning activity must be creative if the enterprise is to achieve efficiency and growth.

Unfortunately, the reality of many companies' marketing planning activities does not match this assumption. Certainly a great deal of time and effort is spent especially on endless 'number-crunching' and budgetary refinement. The effect however is often that the primary purposes of the process are overlooked. Insufficient attention is paid to the search for innovative action, the perspective of the planning team becomes increasingly introverted and when finally the plan is finished, it is little more than a lengthy description of what would have happened anyway.

Unless the plan prescribes the action that should be taken in a way that can be readily implemented and evaluated, it will not be used as a working document by those who have to implement it. Sadly it is the fate of a great number of marketing plans seldom, if ever, to be opened and studied once they have been bound in their glossy covers and placed on the executive bookshelf. If the Marketing Director is to ensure that workable plans are produced at minimum cost and time involvement, he should first check that the company has a sound approach to the planning process and that the planning system reflects the realities of the changing world and the nature of the company and its management attitudes and practices. Having produced the plan, he must review its relevance, coherence and practicality before implementing it as an essential tool for directing and managing the marketing activity.

Approaches to marketing planning

Some companies construct plans at a senior level and delegate them to the more junior management and staff. Other firms start the planning process at the lower levels and consolidate the resulting plans into the overall corporate plan. 'Top-down' planning can ensure that a total corporate view is taken; 'bottom-up' planning that departmental or local experience and expertise is utilized. The most successful approach seems to be a combination of these two methods which can achieve the advantages of both. Such an approach consists of the following stages.

1   Top management refine the corporate marketing, financial and growth objectives and strategies for the forthcoming period taking into consideration the external and internal factors such as the general state of the economies and markets in which they operate, production capability, financial resources of the company, etc. These are issued as planning guidelines to each function of the company. The Marketing Director having played his role as a member of the top management group that decides the basic structure now can start work as leader of the marketing planning team.

2   The planning guidelines are communicated to the lowest possible level in the marketing activity. This can mean both area management and individual salesmen, as well as product or brand management, depending on the structure of the company. The sales wing starts planning by considering the whole product range across the individual territories or markets for which they are responsible; the product or brand managers similarly plan for their particular products or brands. Regular communication needs to be maintained so that each side knows what the other is considering and can take the impact of, for example, new products or local distributive change into account. With such a dual approach, there is a continuous cross-check of forecasts as obviously the totals of sales by both territory and product should ultimately be the same. Furthermore, the involvement of both sides enhances their commitment to the eventual plans that are agreed, thus avoiding the motivational problems caused, for instance, when sales management feel that targets are imposed on them by product or brand management.

3   When the plans have been drafted, the various marketing support

functions – marketing research, sales office, technical service, training – can begin to plan their activities in the light of them. This sequence ensures that the support functions are fully integrated and not allowed to operate as independent units. For example, it can help avoid the common complaint from line sales management that the training departments' programmes have been constructed without full recognition of the present and future realities that face the field sales force.

4   The total marketing plan is brought together and checked for its relevance to and likely achievement of the corporate objectives and strategies, its feasibility and coherence, and the competitive reaction that it may cause. Sufficient time must be allowed at this stage for challenging all or any part of the plan, usually via a process of presentation by the managers concerned to the whole marketing management team led by the Marketing Director, who should play the role of 'devil's advocate'.

This is often the most creative part of the planning process as it forces more detailed analysis and reconsideration or tacitly held assumptions. We find that this challenge phase is often underrated or omitted entirely because of time pressure which usually means that the final plans are not as fully considered as they might have been.

5   When the Marketing Director is satisfied with the marketing plan, it can be circulated and used for detailed production and financial planning. Obviously production and financial considerations will have been built into the original guidelines so that the marketing plan should have taken any major constraints into account. Nevertheless, the consolidation of the marketing and other functional plans often involves further adjustments to each of them before general management can be satisfied that the corporate plan is feasible, challenging and coherent.

If major problems are encountered at this stage, it usually implies that insufficient attention was given to the original planning guidelines. It is very costly and discouraging for the marketing team to be told at this late stage that their plan is not acceptable because there will be insufficient production capacity available or Head Office wants 20 per cent more profit. Such events have become so commonplace in some companies that the planning process has deteriorated into a system of bluff and counterbluff. The marketing team, suspecting that further constraints or demands will be imposed after their plan is completed, deliberately set their figures lower than they know can be achieved in order to create a reserve which can easily be added when the expected final demands are made. In our experience, it is much more effective, less costly and less time-consuming to stretch the planning team at the beginning, not the end, of the whole process and maintain that stretch by rigorous and regular challenge phases during it.

Key factors for a successful marketing planning system

To ensure that the type of approach described above is cost-effective and successful, the Marketing Director should check the points in the following sections.

Innovative planning

The whole marketing planning process should be creative, causing those involved in it to search for growth, more profitable ways of operating, cost reductions, etc. Thus some companies divide the planning process into two stages. First, the planner concerned has to specify what is likely to be achieved in the future assuming the past trends and activities are merely continued. This extrapolation then becomes the planning base upon which the planner is required to improve by creative and productive change. To take a simple example, if sales of a particular product have been growing at 20 per cent p.a. in a company which overall has been expanding at 10 per cent p.a., there is normally little pressure for innovative change upon the product or divisional manager concerned, particularly if the corporate growth objective is, say, 15 per cent. Attention tends to be focused on the sales of the below par products which often by their very nature are the most difficult to increase. By taking the 20 per cent growth trend simply as the planning base and searching for improvements beyond what is already a much above average performance, the manager concerned is encouraged to build on success which is usually much easier and more profitable than attempting to improve below average performance.

In a study of the marketing planning processes of six divisions of a consumer goods group, we were able to demonstrate that the most successful division put the least creative effort into its planning and its plans came under least challenge from corporate management as they could always show a forecast well above average because they were in the fastest growth market of the six involved. Perhaps inevitably, however, because of the lack of pressure upon them, the management team became complacent and when their market eventually became very competitive, they reacted too late and from a weak position which could have been made much stronger if they had planned innovatively earlier.

Standardization

Wherever possible standardized planning formats should be used to ensure that each planner considers the full range of options in a way that enables comparisons and consolidation to be made. This often demands more precise definition of even such basic terms as 'target', 'forecast', 'market' etc. In one case where the word 'potential' had not been defined, it was impossible to consolidate the various departmental plans in the company because some managers had taken it to mean the total existing market of which their sales were part, others that part of the existing market held by competition and yet others the existing market plus what might be available given stronger promotion, better distribution etc.

Table 6.1
Main elements of the marketing plan

Marketing plans usually include:

A statement of basic assumptions with regard to long- and short-term economic, technological, social and political developments.

A review of past sales and profit performance of the company's major products by market and geographic areas.

An analysis of external opportunities and threats by markets and products.

An analysis of the company's and competitors' strengths and weaknesses in facilities, products, finances, customer acceptance, distribution, personnel, pricing, advertising, sales promotion, etc. This analysis will often include assessments of indirect competition.

A statement of long-term objectives (marketing, financial, growth, etc.), and the strategies for achieving them.

A statement of the objectives and strategies for the next year with a detailed breakdown in units and revenue for each product, each market, each geographical area, and each unit of the company's marketing force.

A programme schedule which is carefully co-ordinated with the budgets for the units involved and which shows the sequence of all marketing activities for each product in each market and geographic area so that public relations, advertising, product publicity, sales promotion, and field selling can be co-ordinated.

Statements of objectives for each of the following years similar to the statements for the next year but less detailed.

A summary of how the company intends to capitalize on its opportunities and correct its weaknesses; key priorities, etc.

The elements to be covered by the marketing plan will vary from company to company; Table 6.1 shows a generalized list of headings which can be used as a checklist but which will need additions and deletions to suit the individual firm. There are also books available which give examples of standard planning forms.* Agreement on the headings and formats to be used should be followed by briefing and training for all concerned in the planning process to ensure that they fully understand its objectives and operation. All too often it seems to be assumed that managers know innately why and how to plan and they are left almost entirely to their own devices. It is in such cases of lack of understanding and commitment that the whole planning process tends to become an unwelcome administrative exercise, rather than the vital and creative management function that it should be in any progressive marketing-oriented organization.

Time-span of the plan

Considerable thought needs to be given to the time-span of the plan. Traditionally marketing plans were produced for the year ahead in detail, and three to five years ahead in outline. In an increasingly volatile world these periods may need reconsideration. Even the amount of detail

*For example, John Stapleton, *How to Prepare a Marketing Plan*, Gower, 4th edition, 1988.

demanded in the normal annual plan may now be unrealistic and the time and effort spent on producing it wasted as it is so rapidly outdated. It might be wiser to plan only six months ahead in the traditional detail, leaving the second half of the year to be specified nearer the time.

The medium- and long-term periods certainly should be re-examined for their practicality and shortened wherever possible. Otherwise the planners simply go through the longer-term exercise without any real commitment, knowing that they will have the opportunity to update (which often means totally change!) their three- or five-year plans each year.

Of course, every organization needs a sense of direction for a period of at least a year, but this should be provided by the objectives and strategies. Moreover, some companies, because of the nature of their investments, are forced to take long-term views. However, the Marketing Director can avoid much wasted time if he tailors the plan period to the reality of the changing world and the fundamental corporate needs, rather than continuing traditional practices of lengthy plan periods which today have no real meaning or effect.

The planning cycle

A detailed planning cycle should be laid down specifying the time allowance and deadlines for each stage. Network analysis techniques can be used to ensure that everybody concerned understands the interdependence of the various parts of the plan. Furthermore, such methods can help reduce the total time involved in the planning process. Poor cycle planning causes the twin problems in many companies that the cycle itself is too long and yet the plan never seems to be finished on time.

The first difficulty of a lengthy cycle is that predictions, which on paper are for one year ahead, have to be made six, or even nine months before the beginning of the year in question. As accuracy declines in relation to the length of the forecast period, the longer the cycle, the less valid the plans. If the company's financial year happens to be January 1–December 31 and planning starts in the previous June, it means that the plans for the second half of the next year have to be formulated before the actual results of the corresponding period of the current year are known. Thus much of the prediction tends to be based on the previous year, turning a supposed annual plan into a forecast for two years ahead. Of course, the plan is often updated during such lengthy planning cycles, but the time taken by these drawn-out processes often seems to be greater than the actual implementation activities that they are designed to organize and improve!

Another difficulty is that in some companies top management approval of the plan either in part or in total always seems to be late, sometimes being granted after the beginning of the year in question, and this usually causes an unproductive management reaction. Fearing late approval, the managers concerned tend not to plan significant action in the early part of the plan year in case they do not have time to organize and implement it. Similarly, they may fear that if approval is not granted for the early action, it might destroy the whole basis of their plan. Thus we often find in organizations where late approval has become habitual the so-called annual plan in reality starts two to three months after the beginning of the new year. This is particularly serious when the company's financial year begins at the start of the high-selling season because it can mean that the best time for significant action is lost due to the deficiencies of the planning cycle.

Of course, in large multinational corporations, the planning cycle is necessarily lengthy and complex. Different countries have different seasonal cycles and it is unlikely that a common financial year will match the trading patterns of, for instance, Sweden and Australia. In such circumstances, it is often worth either adopting an overlapping plan concept or subdividing the approval process. The overlapping plan system can be used to plan, for example, 15 months ahead every year so that if approvals are delayed, action can still be taken. This approach also avoids the bifurcation of perception that can be created by the artificiality of the financial year. Although legally trading has to be accounted for up to midnight on say, December 31 and starts again at 00.01 on January 1, in reality of course, it is a continuum which can be too easily ignored within the planning process. Thus the final marketing drive in December to improve this year's results may bring sales forward from the normal January demand causing lower than planned revenue in January and perhaps an intensified and unpredicted competitive reaction.

One of our experiences of subdividing the approval process was in a large multinational where, by the time all the subsidiary plans had been submitted, there was never enough opportunity to challenge them in detail, have them thoroughly reconsidered and then finally approved in time to be put into operation for the new financial year. As top management had decided that the approval deadlines should be maintained, they tended to disregard the challenge process as they knew that it was too late to demand significant change. The other alternative of having the plans submitted earlier would have meant the already lengthy cycle would have had to start even earlier, which again was undesirable. The solution was to divide the marketing planning process into two phases. In the early part of the cycle subsidiaries planned their own objectives, strategies and broad marketing activities within the context of the corporate guidelines which were then reviewed, reconsidered where necessary and approved, at a stage when there was ample time available. Detailed action planning and budgeting then took place so that at the end of the process, the assessment and approval of the total final plan was much simpler and shorter as the overall direction and structure had already been discussed and ratified.

Evaluating the marketing plan

As the plan is gradually constructed and particularly when it is completed, the Marketing Director needs to evaluate it to ensure its relevance to the objectives and strategies of the company, its practicality as a blueprint for implementation and its contribution to the continuing measurement and control of the marketing activity. Reflecting on each of the following aspects will help ensure that the plan achieves the intended goals.

Will it work?

The most basic judgement to be made of any plan is whether its successful implementation will cause the objectives to be achieved. This can be checked by summarizing the key action priorities from what is usually a lengthy document, recognizing that significant changes in results usually demand significant changes in activity. Thus a plan aimed at achieving a 20 per cent sales increase where the only significant change is adding two more salesmen to a force of 50 is unlikely to be successful. Of course, there will normally be statements of how they are all supposed to sell harder and more effectively, but the Marketing Directors might feel such worthy, but un-quantified intentions insufficient, without further significant action such as reorganization of time, training etc. In practice, it is only too easy to be misled by the size and detail of the plan into assuming that enough new significant and relevant action is being taken. A salutary exercise that will often demonstrate this point is to review previous years' plans, the goals they were meant to reach and the actual results that were achieved. All too often, it will be noticed that the generalized statements about trying harder and better are repeated albeit in increasingly elegant phraseology! The Marketing Director must pare the plan down in his analysis to the really new and significant actions, and consider from his experience of similar past activities whether sufficient change has been made and sufficient resources allocated to cause the effects inferred by the corporate objectives. If he is in doubt, he may consider some form of limited experimentation desirable before concluding that the plan is likely to be successful.

Is it consistent?

As he studies the full range of proposed action programmes, the Marketing Director should make sure that they are integrated into a coherent and preferably synergistic whole. For example, plans to eliminate direct servicing of small accounts must be evaluated against intentions to reduce dependence on major customers. Corporate promotion activities must be integrated with in-store merchandizing activity. Pricing changes must be viewed against distributor motivation. Such balancing may seem obvious but it is our experience that because the marketing plan is often produced by a variety of separate managers, it is all too easy to finalize a plan which, at worst, contains mutually contradictory action programmes and even at best fails to gain maximum advantage from the marketing expenditure. This can happen when there is a number of product or brand managers seeking implementation of their plans through common sales, merchandizing, technical service or promotional functions. In such companies, it is often the case that time and effort is spent on fighting for shares of the common resources unless the Marketing Director ensures that there is a fair balance and an effective synthesis inherent in the marketing plan.

Synchronized timing

The timing of the actions within the plan should also be assessed to ensure that it is synchronized and flexible. New product promotion must be preceded by adequate distribution which in turn depends on the briefing and training of the sales force and allowing sufficient time for them to cover their territories adequately. Flexibility implies that sufficient regard has been paid to the length of time it takes to achieve certain actions, with extra to allow for slippage. For example, the time needed to recruit, induct, train and make new management and staff fully effective tends to be under-estimated and little if any allowance made for the effect, for example, of having to re-advertise. If the plan demands an increase in the sales force it is too facile to assume that the new men will be in position and fully operational from the first day of the new year, especially when final plans approval to hire them may only be a few days or weeks before the year starts.

The care needed to synchronize timing within the marketing activity should be redoubled when marketing actions depend on other company functions or outside suppliers. A great deal of effort and tension is wasted trying to adhere to timetables involving others which were probably unrealistic to start with. While understanding the needs and drives of the marketing team to take action as fast as possible, the Marketing Director must recognize that unsynchronized, inflexible and impractical timing can only cause an unproductive use of time or at worst failure to meet critical deadlines. Heavily advertised products that consumers cannot find in stock, industrial sales negotiations whose delivery commitments cannot be met, technical service backlogs reflecting on new product sales are still all common events which might have been eliminated with more realistic analysis of the timing implications of such interrelated actions.

Another aspect of timing that the Marketing Director should check is that the plan does cover the whole period intended. Reference has already been made to the avoidance of action in the early months of the new year caused by recurrent late plans approval. The converse, however, can also obtain where most of the action is taken early in the period covered by the plan, leaving little or no resources for action later on, particularly if unforeseen events occur. Thus in one lingerie company, a three-year marketing plan was constructed for the launch of a new product line specifying the use of 90 per cent of the total promotional expenditure in the first year. This created high demand which unfortunately could not be satisfied because of failure to achieve adequate distribution. However, the heavy advertising alerted the competitors, one of whom responded by rapidly developing and launching their own brand in the second year. This market entry had not been predicted, little promotional reserve was left to counter the launch and the actual sales revenue was lower than predicted because of the failure to supply. By the third year, the competition was totally entrenched and the original company was left a poor second in the market that they had originally identified and developed. Perhaps the story would have ended very differently if the three-year plan had really covered the three years instead of being a one-year plan with two- and three-year sales forecasts based on the assumption of success in the first year.

Competitive action and reaction

The case history above demonstrates another factor which the Marketing Director must ensure has been taken fully into account, that of competitive action and reaction. Although much lip service is paid to monitoring the competition, in practice it seems that management teams can become so introverted during the planning process that they fail to appreciate that any action they plan may not only cause but also condition the competitive response. In one capital equipment firm, detailed plans were formulated for the introduction of an improved product line intended to increase the company's already dominant market share. The new products were superior to all others in the market and it was decided to sell them at a lower price than the main competitor, who traditionally had always had a some-what lower specification, lower price and lower share. By this combination of better products at cheaper prices, the capital equipment firm aimed to sweep the market. They failed to consider that their second place competitor, if he wished to survive at all, had to respond, and as he could not react fast enough by upgrading his product, he was left with the only serious alternative of cutting his prices, thus re-establishing the traditional price relationship but at a lower level. This counteraction maintained the equilibrium of market shares so that the original firm found itself with little sales increase, reduced profit margins and the heavy investment and launch cost of a new product line to be paid for; worst of all perhaps, they had such a lack of self-perception that they blamed the competitor for starting a price war, having put him in a situation where he had no other option!

Because of the problem of failure to recognize likely competitive reactions, it can be worth while, in evaluating the plan, to ask the management team to act out what they would do in the competitor's shoes faced with the series of planned activities. Such simulations can bring a useful perspective to the assessment of the plan and can lead to further improvement, particularly if reactions from other elements of the marketing system are also considered. Reducing the number of distributors, for example, may be perfectly justified by the internal marketing costs savings and activities of the company. What will those distributors do? They will most likely take on other franchises or products. What capital will the competition make out of it? They will probably try to persuade the distributors the company does wish to retain that their turn to be eliminated may be next and therefore they should switch to competitive products now. Such detailed analysis – almost as in playing chess – is necessary to make certain that the marketing plan actions have been thoroughly examined and where necessary reconstructed in the light of predicted external and even internal responses. It may be financially logical to reduce the size of sales representatives' cars but it is likely to be highly demotivational and counterproductive unless the status needs they satisfy are fulfilled simultaneously in some other way.

Evaluation

Finally, the Marketing Director should assure himself that the plan is capable of being constantly evaluated during and particularly at the end of the period it covers. This means that specific goals need to be set for each activity whether these be targets, communication objectives, etc. The actions themselves should be specified, timed and budgeted so that it can be seen what should happen, when, towards what ends at what cost. The executor of each action should be identified, preferably by name, so there can be no misunderstanding about the commitment. Only in this way can the plan be made into a practical prescription for implementation and form a solid basis for the marketing evaluation and control system.

Operating the marketing plan

When the plan is finally 'put to bed' there is normally great relief and rejoicing among marketing management, particularly in those companies where the plan is perceived mainly as a document to satisfy the board or the corporate head office. The attitude of many executives seems to be that once the plan is finalized, they can get back to running the business, implying that planning and implementation are separate and unrelated activities. Perhaps the hardest task for the Marketing Director in the whole planning process is to ensure that such attitudes do not develop, that the planning is not perceived as separate from (and interfering with) the managerial function and, most important of all, that the completion and approval of the plan is the beginning, not the end, of the planning process. Patently if the plan is not used as a marketing tool by management, the cost, time and effort that goes into its construction is largely wasted. The Marketing Director must make it absolutely clear that the plan is to be a practical document, that it will be used to implement and control the marketing activity and will form a basis for individual performance evaluation of the managers concerned. Such attitudes must be inculcated during the planning cycle and especially throughout the implementation process.

This can be achieved by scheduling regular review meetings at at least quarterly intervals when the action programmes specified in the plan will be discussed to ensure they have been implemented and to assess the results that have accrued from them. Any additions or amendments to the plan in the light of unforeseen or changing circumstances can be decided and noted in writing on the plan document itself. This is particularly important so that when the next planning cycle commences, there is a more realistic basis available. From time to time, and at least annually, the longer-term plans from previous years should be evaluated. Even in those companies which do carefully monitor the progress of the annual plan, it is rare to find sufficient assessment of the three-year plan of two years ago.

This emphasis on ensuring the use and evaluation of plans does not imply that they will be perfect prescriptions which must be followed without question. It is because plans do have to be changed in the light of unpredicted and unpredictable events that such reviews are so important. If the planning process is to be improved and made even more valuable as a management tool, the Marketing Director needs to determine why unpredicted events were overlooked, why action programmes did not achieve the desired results, why apparently feasible timetables were not met and why previous longer-term forecasts were so unrealistic two years later. He must consider whether the whole planning approach needs modification, whether the planning system has weaknesses, or whether the people concerned are insufficiently skilled or motivated.

Only by such pressure for improvement can the Marketing Director ensure that the whole marketing planning activity fulfils its goals. It should be a highly practical, creative process which specifies the actions needed to achieve the objectives of the company via the designated strategies. It should be an integral part of the managerial function providing clear programmes for action and criteria for evaluation of both company and individual performance.

Successful companies 'plan the work and work the plan', recognizing that the quality of the work is improved by good planning and the quality of the planning is improved by regular assessment of the work. It should be the aim of every Marketing Director to achieve such apparently simple goals yet there will be few honest ones who do not have from time to time an uneasy feeling that their planning processes are an expensive way of producing elegant statements of what would have happened anyway, and in a form which is never fully used to implement and control the marketing activity.

CHECKLIST

1   *Approaches to marketing planning*

1.1   Do we have a clear concept of the marketing planning activity specifying its goals and processes?
1.2   Does our approach ensure that clear guidelines are given?
1.3   Do we gain the advantages of both the corporate view and local experience?
1.4   Is marketing planning well integrated with the other functional planning processes in the organization?
1.5   Are there sufficient opportunities for 'challenge' built into our approach?

2   *Key factors for a successful marketing planning system*

2.1   Does our system encourage creative and innovative planning?
2.2   Do we have sufficiently standardized formats?
2.3   Have all concerned in planning been given enough briefing and training?
2.4   Have we recently reconsidered the time-spans for the plans?
2.5   Do we have a well constructed planning cycle?

3   *Evaluating the marketing plan*

3.1   How do we decide that there is sufficient action planned to achieve our objectives?
3.2   Are our plans well integrated and synergistic?
3.3   Is the timing synchronized and flexible where necessary?
3.4   Are the actions and reactions of competition, distribution and even elements of our own company thoroughly considered?
3.5   Is the plan constructed so that it can be readily implemented and results evaluated against it?

4   *Operating the marketing plan*

4.1   Do we review performance against plan thoroughly and regularly enough?
4.2   How do we ensure that our planning improves?
4.3   Is planning seen as an essential, practical and integral part of the managerial function?
4.4   Is the plan used to evaluate individual as well as corporate performance?
4.5   Overall, do we 'plan the work and work the plan' as effectively as we should?

Chapter 7

Building an Effective Marketing Organization

The fundamental purpose of the marketing organization structure is to utilize the marketing resources (notably the people) in the most cost-effective manner to achieve the objectives of the company. Simple though it is to state, it seems often very difficult to achieve in practice. While good structures are not the sole reason for marketing success, it is certainly worth the time of the Marketing Director to reflect on the precise goals he wishes to achieve with his organization, the different considerations that have to be balanced within it and what kind of structure will optimize the use of resources.

He should recognize even before starting such a review, however, that any structural solution is bound to be a compromise between the conflicting pressures of the marketplace, the products, the cost-effective use of the company's resources and the human responses of the individuals concerned. Acceptance that there is no perfect solution perhaps might prevent the over-frequent changes that some companies seem to suffer. They appear to be striving for perfection where none is attainable and even if it were, it would not be the panacea that they seem to expect.

Evolution of marketing organization structure

A study of the evolution of marketing organization structure soon demonstrates the need for changing responses to external and internal pressures and can serve as a useful starting point for the Marketing Director's review. Often understanding why the current structure is as it is can give useful clues to its improvements. Essentially the structural

100

evolution consists of five stages, not all exemplified in every organization and often with modifications in individual companies. Nevertheless there is a general pattern of transition in structures reflecting the forced change in attitude from production orientation through sales orientation to marketing orientation. Figure 7.1 illustrates these stages.

Stage 1. The early history of most companies is characterized by an excess of demand over production, a focusing of attention therefore on the manufacturing or buying side of the company and a simple sales structure for communicating and distributing the products or services to the market. Typically the major and often the only communication mechanism used was personal field selling on a territory basis, and the whole purpose of the structure was to sell what was made.

Stage 2. As the means of supply usually expand faster than the means of consumption inevitably production begins to overtake demand. As that happens, it becomes noticeably more difficult to sell what the factory makes; the typical response is to intensify the sales activity.

At this stage, other persuasive communication mechanisms such as advertising and sales promotion are used increasingly. Marketing research may also be employed if only to try to find out why selling has become so much more difficult. Although in terms of stance, the company has only become sales-oriented, this may be masked by titular changes, e.g. the Sales Director overnight becoming the Marketing Director. These attempts to continue the company's success by intensifying the sales effort, although they alleviate, they do not usually solve the underlying problem which is that no amount of promotion will sell products in the long term if they do not match the changing consumer needs. Furthermore, by this stage the marketing expenditure per product has often reached a level where it is felt that more control is needed than can be given by the traditional sales management processes; moreover the existing managers usually lack experience or expertise in the new promotional methods.

Stage 3. This is normally the phase when some kind of marketing activity first appears as an addition to the existing sales structure. Recognizing the deficiencies in activity and expertise of the traditional sales structure and staff, 'marketing' is introduced alongside it, sometimes leading up to the new position of Marketing Director. The marketing function is perceived largely as a planning and control activity often focused on the products. The intention is to ensure that the products are more oriented to market requirements and that all expenditure (notably on promotion) is brought under the control of particular individuals. The sales activity is left as an implementation organization usually still on a territorial basis.

The major weakness of such structures is the artificial division between 'marketing' and 'sales' particularly where two directors are concerned. In practice the Sales Director by dint of his age and experience is seen as the

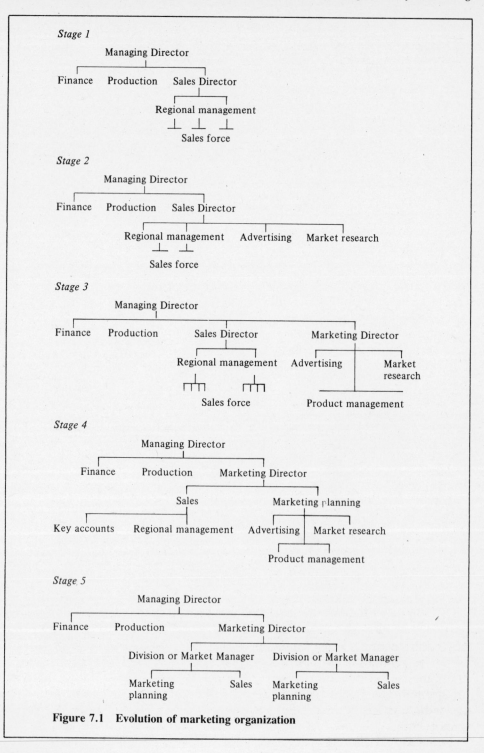

Figure 7.1   Evolution of marketing organization

senior but the newer Marketing Director, by virtue of deciding the plans, in effect controls the sales activity. At a lower level in the structure, there is often conflict between various product managers, striving for more concentration on their particular products, and the sales force, acting as a common resource to all of them.

Stage 4.   Most companies recognize sooner or later (often after a degree of political in-fighting) that there is an essential integration in the marketing concept and that sales is simply one, albeit perhaps the most important, of the major tactics by which marketing plans are implemented. Thus at this stage the Sales Director position tends to be eliminated; that is not to say the incumbent of the job disappears. We have seen a number of cases where wily old Sales Directors become sole Marketing Directors in this phase!

The planning and implementation wings of the structure are thus drawn together under a single head. Other changes are often made at this stage as the company perceives more clearly the total change from 'what can we make and how can we sell it?' to 'what can we sell and how can we make it?'.

Viewing the company through the eyes of the marketplace looking inward, rather than through the eyes of the factory looking ouward often causes reconsideration of the sales structure which interfaces with the customers. Thus major accounts, or different industries, may be singled out for particular sales attention.

The problem of this type of organization (which is still very common) is that delegation of profit responsibility below the Marketing Director is very difficult because no other level has total responsibility and authority for any aspect of the marketing activity. Furthermore, doubts begin to grow about whether the product or brand manager concept is sufficiently marketing-oriented. The structure tends to encourage these managers to over-concentrate on selling their current products or brands, rather than satisfying the needs of the marketplace. Thus, if a need could be better satisfied by a totally different mechanism, would the product manager recognize it, particularly if it might imply his own elimination? For instance, in an agricultural equipment company, the product manager in charge of ploughs overlooked the significant developments in chemical farming which in certain soil conditions totally obviate the need for mechanical cultivation. Not surprisingly, if erroneously, he perceived his job as selling ploughs, not as satisfying the market for soil preparation.

Stage 5.   To make the marketing organization more marketing-oriented and to overcome the problem of delegation of profit responsibilities, many companies have moved totally or partially to a market-based structure. In such organizations, all the functions of planning and implementation are focused on a market or groups of markets. This can mean that each Market Manager has his own planning team and even his own sales force, particularly if discrete customer groups or distribution channels are involved. Even where there is still a common sales force, product or brand management teams may be reorganized on a market basis. Thus a toiletries company has changed its traditional product group management structure to a format which focuses attention on its three major markets of hair, skin and teeth.

The advantage of such an evolution is that marketing management is given the wider task of achieving results from a market, not simply from the current range of products. It broadens the spectrum of search for new and profitable need satisfiers. Furthermore, it allows real profit responsibility to be identified and delegated market by market, particularly where there are separate sales forces.

No doubt marketing organization structures will continue to evolve as they attempt to respond cost-effectively to the changing needs of the marketplace and the changing demands of corporate objectives and strategies. In those industries where distribution patterns have become highly polarized, some companies are begining to reconstruct their organizations around the major accounts, treating them almost as one-customer markets.

One industrial company has created a special marketing department to deal solely with British Steel, separate from the rest of its general engineering business. A number of food companies see such developments as a natural evolution from the traditional key accounts sales activity, expanding the scope of that process to include research, product planning, advertising, sales promotion, merchandising etc., thus constructing a microcosmic marketing function to handle the individual major national account. However, such concentration can give rise to other problems of organization. For example, although it is relatively easy to regroup head office functions in this way, should the field salesmen who deal with the local offices or branches of the national account be controlled by regional sales management or by the national key account activity?

At a supranational level, the growing complexities of international business have outdated traditional 'home and export' organizational concepts. There has been a general trend away from satisfying each market by local manufacturing towards a separation of the activities of production and marketing. Manufacturing units are tending to become larger and concentrated on more limited product ranges so that competitive economies of scale can be achieved. Furthermore, they are being relocated or developed in lower-cost countries. The expansion of motor manufacturing in Spain by multinational corporations at a level far beyond the requirements of the Spanish domestic market is but one example of a trend in many industries such as footwear, textiles and electronics.

The criteria for the location and scale of manufacturing are thus becoming increasingly different from those used in judging the nature and structure of the marketing activity. The marketing organization must be capable of identifying and satisfying not only the demands of one particular country, but also the common needs between markets which can be met by similar products and promotion. This has led some companies to separate the sales and distribution activities, which usually remain a national responsibility, from the marketing planning and product management function which needs to become increasingly international.

The structuring of international marketing activity, however, tends to be highly complex as it must recognize both the similarities and differences between various countries. For example, should European marketing management and planning be based on geographical, economic, language, cultural, ethnic or legal characteristics? Can the four countries of the Nordic region be treated as a geographical group when only Denmark is a member of the EC, only Norway produces oil, Finland has its own distinct language and Sweden's industrial structure is totally different from those of the other three? Thus each country must be treated individually to a degree, but for many industries not one of these markets is large enough to justify its own special product range and therefore common factors must be found. It is this need to balance national and supranational requirements that is causing much rethinking of international marketing structures.

Reviewing the existing organization

It is against this constantly evolving background that the Marketing Director should reconsider his structure from time to time. Such reviews should be conducted systematically, working from the national and international marketplace inwards. Although it may seem self-evident that a marketing organization should reflect the needs and mechanisms of the markets that it is trying to satisfy, in practice we often find organizational redesign starts at board level and works downwards. This almost invariably means that the resulting structure is designed more for the needs of the company and the individuals within it than the markets that it is attempting to supply. To avoid such dangers, the following steps should be followed in sequence.

Defining the tasks to be performed

In Part I of this book, emphasis was laid on the importance of specifying all the elements of the market system and comprehending how each currently worked. If the marketing organization is to be able to satisfy profitably the needs of consumers, distributors and, where relevant, customers, with its products/price/promotion mix, then it must be capable of three funda-mental tasks:

1 The collection and analysis of data, both quantitative and qualitative, about each element of the market system and how it is changing.
2 The planning of appropriate product price and promotional activity which will competitively satisfy each element.
3 The implementation of such plans by the marketing organization itself (e.g. selling), by outside agencies (e.g. advertising) and by other functions of the company (e.g. manufacturing the products to quality and delivery standards).

Each of these categories should be described in detail, specifying the priorities of the task to be performed, estimating how much work is involved and whether it is best performed by company staff or external help. Thus the general data collection and analysis task might need refocusing on distributor research and the examination of key overseas markets. The work involved may be best controlled by one person supported by specialist agencies, especially for the foreign research. Likewise, the sales task might require redefinition in the light of the changing nature and scale of the customers. Whereas traditionally the sales effort might have been spread geographically, this may no longer be appropriate if a small number of accounts dominates the market and the rest are becoming increasingly uneconomic to service by personal selling.

Concentrating on the nature of the task to be performed, rather than the traditional means of performing it, can also lead to the development of more cost-effective solutions. For example, a time-consuming part of the sales task may be routine order taking which, although traditionally handled by a salesman, may be equally well but more cheaply performed by telephone selling or even computer link-up.

By the end of this first stage of the organizational review, therefore, the Marketing Director should be better able to answer the key questions:

1   What are the tasks to be performed to identify and satisfy the various needs of the market system?
2   What is the most cost-effective way of performing those tasks?

Grouping the tasks to be performed

The process of organization has been described as the grouping together of like activities. Traditionally this has been on the basis of the similarities of the tasks to be performed and the most economic way in which they can be carried out. The classic sales force structure exemplifies these principles. If the sales task is to sell to customers at the lowest possible cost, dividing the country into geographical territories each capable of being handled by one person is the best solution. However, it assumes that all customers in a territory require essentially similar servicing and that servicing costs are the primary yardstick for judging organizational performance.

The marketing organization should not be evaluated in terms of cost alone, but by the relationship between the costs incurred and the revenue and profit generated. Furthermore, the key similarities around which tasks should be grouped may be found not simply within the company's own activities, but more meaningfully in the marketplace that the organization is designed to service. Thus the sales force structure is usually more effective if it is based on the common factors among customer requirements. This implies a deeper examination of the nature of the different types of customers, what kind of sales effort will be most persuasive to each, the range of sales skills that can be expected from any one individual, and therefore how customer groupings can be defined based on like characteristics.

Such reviews have led companies to many different conclusions about the relevant customer categories and thus the most effective sales force structure. Common groupings are by industry, customer size (e.g. separating key accounts) customer type (e.g. handling specifiers such as architects separate from contractors), customer usage (dividing original equipment purchases from distributors supplying the replacement market), and sales task (e.g. separating prospecting from routine servicing). Many firms use a combination of two or more structures recognizing, for example, the essential differences between both the industries they serve and the large and small customers within each industry.

The grouping together of the planning tasks should be approached in a similar way. Historically the most common focal point has been the product or brand. This has the advantage of ensuring that all activities, revenues and costs are planned and controlled by one person, but its value as a reflection of the marketplace has already been questioned. Many firms have concluded that there are more effective forms of planning and controlling the marketing activity based on the concept of 'market' management. This can mean management by consumer market segment (as in the hair, skin and teeth example quoted earlier), industry (e.g. an industrial manufacturer has grouped its planning activities around the major industries it serves such as automotive, steel, paper manufacturing etc.), or by distribution channel (e.g. separating the grocery from the chemist trade). Again, combinations of approach can be employed depending on the nature of the planning and control tasks. Some firms have evolved a matrix management approach utilizing both product and market management (see Figure 7.2). However, unless it is decided in advance that one is senior to the other, it is our experience that serious operational problems can arise because it is unclear who should take the ultimate decisions.

Grouping the tasks of the marketing activity into the most cost-effective structure is probably the most difficult organizational decision facing the

	Market Manager A	Market Manager B	Market Manager C
Product Manager X			
Product Manager Y			
Product Manager Z			

Figure 7.2 Matrix organization for marketing

Marketing Director as there is usually a wide range of options. There will seldom be any one format which can be uniformly applied across the whole range of marketing planning and implementation activities and which will combine maximum effectiveness and minimum cost. However, it should be possible to construct the best compromise from a logical and sequential approach.

This should start with identifying the focal points of the consumer or end-user markets on the satisfaction of which the company ultimately depends. This grouping, whether by market segment or industry, should form the basis for the planning activity involving specification of consumer needs, product development, pricing and promotional strategies.

Second, depending on the product range, technical complexity and promotional activities required, this market planning activity may need to include or be supported by product or brand management or research or promotion specialists.

Third, the grouping of the sales function should be considered. Wherever feasible, this should mirror the planning structure as this facilitates communications and control. Often, however, this is not possible because the sales structure has to mirror the distributors or customers with whom it deals, and these may have common characteristics different from the end-user market, which may be the prime basis for structuring the planning activity.

Fourth, within the overall sales activity groupings, whether based on geography, industry, customer size etc., the organization of the various sales tasks must be decided. These will normally include receiving enquiries, finding new customers, regular order taking, order processing and after-sales servicing, plus in some companies activities such as technical advice and merchandising. The Marketing Director has to judge which and how many of these tasks should be performed by the field sales personnel, recognizing that the salesman's skills may not stretch to technical advice nor his time to monitoring order processing. It is wise, therefore, to concentrate the very expensive field sales time on those jobs that can only be performed by the field salesman (e.g. finding and persuading new customers) and supporting him in the other tasks with sales office personnel, telephone selling, technical advisory staff, merchandisers, etc.

Matching the organization structure to corporate priorities

By following the approach described so far, the Marketing Director should have constructed an organization capable of handling the planning and implementation tasks of the marketing activity. However, there remains the problem in most companies of ensuring that enough commitment and resources support activities which may today be minor or ineffective, but could and should be significant in the future. These can include new products, new markets, new distribution channels, diversification opportunities or simply potential blockages in the marketing system. As short-term results inevitably gain more attention than long-term prospects, specific organizational positions may be needed to ensure the appropriate balance is achieved. This may mean separating the product and/or market development processes from the basic marketing planning activity and committing particular individuals to managing them. For example, in a packaging company, the marketing development process was established centrally separate from the operating divisions and given the task of developing new products either to satisfy existing needs better or new needs that the firm had not identified in the past. This corporate unit was also responsible for finding the first three customers for any new development after which they handed over the wider-scale marketing to the relevant operating subsidiary. This organizational separation of the development activity caused a large increase in the number of new products brought successfully to the marketplace.

In a food company, the establishment of an organization position focused entirely on the search for channel diversification led to a significant and desirable broadening of the firm's distributive base. A multinational capital equipment corporation recognized that many of its sales activities, especially in Third World countries, depended increasingly on funding from international sources such as the World Bank, the EC and the IMF. It therefore created a top-level position wholly responsible for maintaining positive contact with such sources, communicating with the appropriate line sales organizations around the world and generally ensuring that the corporation's future sales expansion was not inhibited by the buyer's lack of finance.

In each of these cases, the opportunity or the problem was identified as significant but insoluble within the context of the general organization structure. By committing senior managers wholly to the tasks, solutions were found. It is doubtful that such approaches could have been successful with lower-level appointments, although that is a common organizational response. A typical instance is where a company launches a totally new product line and tries to market it through its existing structure recognizing that it is different only by appointing, say, a new brand manager and perhaps a new salesman per region. Although this gains junior staff commitment, the whole middle and top management structure still has to direct and manage the existing business as well as the new product. If, for example, the new line is targeted even at 10 per cent of the total business, this means that 90 per cent of the results must be achieved from the existing products. Not surprisingly 90 per cent of management time will be spent on the ongoing activities despite the fact that 10 per cent of management time is probably insufficient to cause a new product to achieve its 10 per cent target. We suspect that ineffective resolution of this dilemma is a key reason for failure of new ventures and new products.

It is often the case that unless a company is prepared to commit organizational resources to new developments until they are strong enough to be absorbed, the chances of success are low. The best way of ensuring results is to commit one or more senior managers in such a way that they cannot retreat into the current business activities. Such commitment need not of course be permanent. Secondment to development or problem activities is a powerful means of increasing resources. Furthermore, external help can be used, especially for short-term situations, for example, supplementing the existing field force with commando sales teams for effective widescale new product launching, using consulants to analyse and resolve particular blockages or research agencies to help identify new market opportunities.

Deciding how many people are needed

Having identified the nature and grouping of the tasks to be performed the Marketing Director must decide how many managers and staff are needed to carry them out. He must weigh the inevitably high cost against the desired effectiveness. All costs connected with personnel are rising – recruitment, remuneration, social security contributions, office services and even termination. Many of them are likely to increase even faster as the UK harmonizes its legislation and practices with the rest of the EC.

It is well known that salary levels are considerably higher in most European countries than in the UK; what is less well recognized is that in some countries social security charges are already over 40 per cent of annual remuneration or that dismissal for any reason short of criminal may have to be compensated by up to two years' salary! Thus every Marketing Director should consider very deeply how few rather than how many people he needs.

Starting with the sales division of the organization as this usually contains the largest number of people, the first decision will be to reassess the number of salesmen required. Although some companies try to decide this on the basis of sales potential or revenue, the only logical approach is to assess how much work there is to be done and thus how much time it will occupy. The only common factor between salesmen (and indeed between all employees) is the number of hours they are supposed to work. A simple method for calculating the appropriate sales force using this workload concept is shown in Table 7.1.

Because of the reducing number of buying points in both consumer and industrial markets and increasing automation of the ordering process, it is likely that sales force sizes will decrease in most industries, a reduction that will be accelerated by the increasing imbalance between sales servicing costs and potential revenue from smaller customers.

In some cases less expensive sales office or telephone selling staff will be used for such small customer servicing; in others they will have to be handled via some form of distributive network. If these tasks are to be carried out by company personnel, again the workloads need to be quantified before the number of people required can be calculated.

Having decided the number of different types of sales staff, the number of managers needed has to be assessed. General hypotheses of spans of control are of little use; it is much sounder to estimate from a list of managerial tasks the workload of the manager and thus how many staff he can control. Table 7.2 shows an example of such a calculation.

Table 7.1
Calculating sales force size

$$\frac{\text{Number of actual and potential customers x Call frequency}}{\text{Average daily call rate x Number of working days per year}}$$

Customer categories and call frequencies
Category *A* (over £50,000 a year)   500 x 12 visits p.a. =   6,000
Category *B* (£25,000–£50,000 a year) 2,000 x   9 visits p.a. = 18,000
Category *C* (£10,000–£25,000 a year) 5,000 x   6 visits p.a. = 30,000
Category *D* (under £10,000 a year)   7,000 x   2 visits p.a. = <u>14,000</u>

                                      Annual call total 68,000

Average daily call rate = 8
Number of working days
    Total days in year   365
    Weekends   104
    Holidays   15
    Sickness   5
    Training   10
    Conferences   5
    Meetings   <u>11</u>   <u>150</u>
Number of working days   215
Call total per salesman 215 x 8   = 1,720

Number of salesmen required = $\dfrac{68,000}{1,720}$ = 40 salesmen

Table 7.2
Example of sales management workload assessment

			Workload calculation		
1 Sales management responsibilities	Final selection of staff Organization Field training Motivation Control Other staff provide: recruitment sales promotion sales administration	Because of services provided, manager needs only 1 day a week in office	Average working month Office 4 days Meetings 1 day Personal selling 4 days	21 days <u>9 days</u>	<u>12 days</u>
	Sales manager meeting	1 day a month	Must spend 1½ days per man a month ∴ can manage 8 men		
2 Nature of sales task	Repeat selling of consumable product to industrial buyer. Little prospecting				
3 Amount of personal selling by manager	Manager personally sells to big customers on territory. Also helps salesmen with their larger customers	About 4 days a month About ½ day per salesman a month			
4 Degree of field training necessary	Relatively new team needing regular field training	About 1 day per salesman a month			

A similar approach can be used at each level in the sales management hierarchy, although admittedly it is more difficult to assess workload and time utilization at more senior levels as the tasks themselves are less easily quantified. However, the numbers of positions concerned are much smaller and the judgements usually simpler. Whereas it can be a complex process to decide whether 50 salesmen is the appropriate number, usually there is only one choice about how many General Sales Managers are needed.

Deciding numbers on the marketing planning and support side of the organization is somewhat more complex. Here it is recommended that the number of market or product managers is established first as these represent the basic modules of the marketing planning activity within each market or product area. The workload can then be evaluated to decide whether there is sufficient work for one person; if not, one manager may be able to handle two or more products or markets. If there is more work than can be handled by one person, it has to be assessed whether each should have his own support staff or whether similar tasks should be removed and given to a separate functional manager (e.g. sales promotion activities).

Any other corporate priorities as discussed in the previous section will need to be considered. Usually they are few but require senior people, ideally with very few staff reporting to them. Otherwise, not only will the personal time be diverted from their particular priority into administration and supervision, but also they will be less motivated to cause their work to be absorbed as quickly as possible into the general marketing organization.

Finally the Marketing Director should consider his own workload and time utilization. If he has too many people reporting to him or too many personal tasks, he will not have 'thinking time' which all senior executives seem to crave. At least the opportunity for such time can be created by appropriate structural decisions; whether that potential is realized will depend on the quality of his immediate subordinates and his own self-discipline.

Marketing structures have tended to grow, often vastly, in numbers as well as cost as they have evolved from simple sales functions attached to production-oriented enterprises to international marketing-oriented organizations. Although it is inevitable and appropriate that the numbers of managers and staff have increased, many senior executives in other functions, as well as general managers, seem very concerned about the present size of their marketing organizations. It is therefore very much in the Marketing Director's personal interest as well as that of his company to evaluate regularly the number of people in his structure and particularly to assess their cost-effectiveness. At least this may prevent the dreaded 'head-count' limitations being imposed upon him. This crude management control often reduces effectiveness out of proportion to cost saving as it tends to eliminate junior staff leaving their work to be done by more senior, more expensive management.

Integrating the marketing organization within the company

The marketing organization does not of course operate independently. It is involved with R and D, production and finance. In an integrated marketing-oriented company, R and D will need market data to guide its activities towards developing products that are saleable, production scheduling must obviously be closely integrated with sales forecasting and order processing, pricing activities will to a degree depend on costing information from the finance function, etc.

It is often at these points that organizational failure occurs. In a carpet company we discovered the seemingly paradoxical, but frighteningly common situation of a large sales order book with extended delivery dates, an under-utilized factory, and a warehouse full of stock. This had been caused by the lack of an organizational structure and system to link together sales forecasting, order receipt and progressing, production scheduling, stocking and distribution. Moreover, it was very unclear where the responsibility and authority lay. The sales manager assumed he should maximize sales and thus took all the orders he could for any item in a vast range of carpet patterns, colours and sizes. The production manager was trying to optimize factory efficiency by making long runs once the looms had been set up, an expensive and time-consuming process. The warehouse manager tried to accept and store the finished stock as best he could, but could not ship it out because the orders held did not match the products available.

This typical situation of different functions trying to achieve their individual objectives (especially when these are not clearly specified and integrated) and in the process causing corporate problems, requires in part at least an organizational solution. This must start with a precise identification of the tasks to be performed and the responsibilities and authority for those tasks, especially at the interface between functions. In this case, the approach adopted was to arrange a better data exchange between marketing and production so that sales could plan to sell, knowing what was likely to be available, and production could plan to make what was likely to be sold. The Marketing Director was given the authority to ask for changes in the production schedule to meet particular and important customer needs even though such changes caused reduction in production runs and thus an increase in cost. He had, however, to take the financial responsibility for variances against standard costs caused by his requests. Furthermore, he was given responsibility for finished stock levels to encourage sales effort behind those products already in stock.

The need to construct and maintain an integrated and balanced process of sales, production and distribution and ensure the optimal cost-effectiveness of each function and the system as a whole might appear too obvious and too elementary to be worthy of discussion in a book intended for top management. However, it is our consistent experience even in so-called sophisticated companies that this fundamental organizational process needs reviewing from time to time. It is particularly necessary where the various functions are located on different sites – a more and more frequent occurrence both nationally and internationally. In the case of multinational operations where the placing of production units is decided by very different criteria from those which govern the location and organization of

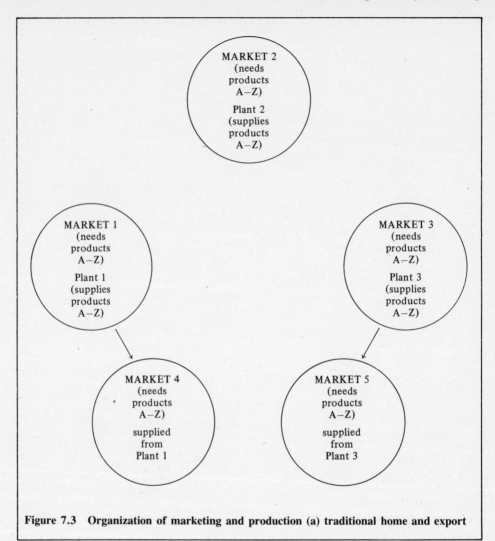

Figure 7.3   Organization of marketing and production (a) traditional home and export

marketing activities, if often demands the creation of a stronger logistics function to bring the two together.

For example, where each national production facility is concentrated on a small part of the product range in order to achieve economies of scale, but each market requires the full range to satisfy local demand, the problem of balancing country sales forecasts with production schedules and physical distribution becomes extremely complex. In one pan-European company, a separate central forecasting and supply function had to be created to manage this interface. Into this data could be fed on a market basis covering all products and translated into production schedules aggregating demand for the various parts of the product range manufactured by the different plants. Furthermore, the warehousing and distribution function had to be restructured, particularly to serve smaller overseas markets which traditionally had been supplied with the whole range from one plant. Given that no

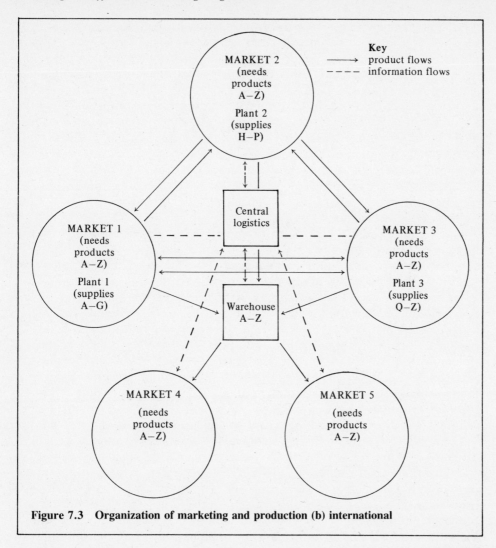

Figure 7.3   Organization of marketing and production (b) international

one factory now makes the whole range, the alternative to duplicating many times over the distribution function in respect of, say, an African market, was to establish central warehousing on a continental scale. Such a warehouse could thus make up a full range shipment to the market from the different outputs of the various plants. Figure 7.3 shows the evolution of such structures as a company moves from national to international marketing and production.

Another key relationship is that between marketing and finance. If the marketing activity is to fulfil its task of supplying value satisfactions at a profit, obviously it needs financial data on which to base decisions about production introduction and elimination, judgements about customer profitability, pricing strategies and tactics, etc. Frequently, however the structure of the financial function and systems makes it difficult to produce information in the appropriate format. For example, although many companies can produce cost information by product, few can accurately identify all the cost elements by customer, which can be vital, especially in key account negotiation. Such problems might be overcome by installing new systems; some companies however perceive the need for financial information and awareness within the marketing activity as so important that they adopt the structural solution of creating a financial position within the marketing function. The Marketing Controller, as he is often called, usually reports to the Marketing Director and is responsible for identifying the financial implications of marketing activities, specifying what financial data are needed for marketing decision making, liaising with the finance function to ensure that accurate information is produced on time in a usable format, and generally advising on all financial aspects of marketing objectives, strategies and tactics.

Analogous structural solutions may improve the relationship of the marketing organization with other corporate activities. For instance, in some companies with large sales forces and thus significant problems of recruitment, remuneration, appraisal, development and even termination in an environment made increasingly complex by legislation and unionism, the function of Sales Personnel Manager has been created. The introduction of such positions recognizes the need for full-time professional expertise in personnel and employee relations. Moreover, it helps eliminate the many difficulties between, for example, sales management and the personnel department, particularly where personnel is perceived to be largely 'works'-oriented and totally unfamiliar with the particular and often peculiar problems of the sales force.

Interface problems occur in every organization because in practice the individual goals of the various functions are sometimes in conflict with each other, even where clear corporate objectives have been specified. In rapidly changing markets the current manufacturing capability is often not precisely in line with the needs of the consumers. The marketing activity strives to have made what can be most easily and profitably sold. The production function attempts to have sold what can be most easily and profitably manufactured. Both attitudes are justifiable individually, but unless a balanced compromise is reached, neither function will reach its goals. Most general managers of course recognize their responsibility for arbitrating such conflicts. What has been suggested above, however, is that there may be structural approaches which can alleviate if not eliminate some of these difficulties.

It would be wrong to imply that any such structural solutions are likely to be panaceas. Better systems, improved communications and management development can all be equally powerful approaches to these interface difficulties; these aspects are considered in the next chapter which deals with the running of the marketing organization.

The fact that structural initiatives are being implemented by various companies is, however, not only a recognition of the importance of creating an organization that can run efficiently, but also an indication of the evolution of organization theory. Whereas traditionally an organization might have been constructed around the grouping of like functions to minimize expense, it is now being recognized as a decision-making system capable of planning and operating cost-effectively in an increasingly complex and changing environment.

Redesigning a marketing organization structure – a case history

The experience of one of our clients in metal manufacturing demonstrates a number of the key issues in deciding the marketing organization structure.

The company had a record of wide fluctuation in its profitability caused by the cyclical nature of its industry. To try to establish a steadier growth pattern, it was decided to review the long-term marketing objectives and strategies of the company. This led to the conclusion that future consistent profit growth could only be achieved by identifying and selecting markets or segments of markets that themselves demonstrated steady growth at attractive price levels as well as other criteria such as stable distribution patterns, low competitive threat from substitution products, etc.

Even as the exercise commenced, it was clear that the existing organization structure could neither produce the relevant data nor plan and implement market-related activity. It consisted of a domestic sales activity based on handling large customers direct and small customers through a variety of distribution networks, the latter sales force being organized on a geographic basis. There was also an export sales team. The planning of the marketing activity was structured on a product manager basis, although in some cases particular products were only used by particular markets, so it might be argued that the Product Manager concerned was also a Market Manager. In an extreme case, one customer represented the whole market for a particular product, thus the Product Manager was also Market Manager and Key Account Manager! There was, however, no clear recognition or definition in the company of what constituted a 'product', a 'market' or a 'customer'.

A major study of the various markets and their segments that the company could and/or did serve demonstrated that there were two broad categories: 'A' markets that could be specified by both customer need and product specification, and 'B' markets that could only be defined by product. An example of an 'A' market was the defence industry which needs metals combining particular strength and lightness. 'B' markets were those where different types of metals were required for reprocessing into a vast variety of end products for industrial and consumer use.

The marketing activity needed for success in these two categories of markets differed. 'A' markets could be planned and managed on a market base, with a sales activity direct to end-user. Moreover, the five key 'A' markets identified tended to operate internationally. The defence industry again demonstrates the point; military requirements and their satisfaction are largely international in both demand and supply. The 'B' markets on the other hand were national in that each country had a different manufacturing profile usually served by different types of distributive networks. Generally it was uneconomic to attempt to serve large numbers of small reprocessors direct and distribution channels had to be selected and used. Because 'A' markets were easier and more profitable to access and control, the company chose a long-term strategy of continuously attempting to identify new 'A'-type markets emerging from the 'B' category. This meant the twin functions of product and market development needed to be established.

The final organizational consideration was that although it seemed clear that the two classifications of markets needed to be operated separately, there were some marketing activities common to both of them, e.g. order processing, export documentation and shipping, corporate promotion, etc. Furthermore, the market categorization did not match the production organization. There were two factories each only capable of making products for some of both the 'A' and 'B' markets. Thus there was a need for a central liaison function with production scheduling at each plant to avoid the potential interface problems.

Taking into account all these factors, a new structure was designed (see Figure 7.4). This reflected much more clearly the nature of the markets to be served by dividing the marketing organization into two divisions. Within the 'A' markets' division, market managers plan, implement and control all the necessary marketing and sales activity internationally. In the 'B' markets' division there is a strong sales function organized basically for home and export with sales activities organized geographically selling through distribution networks. Growing markets are identified and exploited by the market development function; expanding products by the product development function, thus giving considerable commitment to future growth. When, through these twin processes, a market can be specified clearly enough, it can then become an 'A' market. The common services and production interface functions are not split but handled by a central marketing services function.

This case history is not intended to demonstrate a perfect organizational solution; it has already been stated that any structure by its nature is a compromise. An experienced Marketing Director will quickly identify potential problems inherent in this structure. Such problems might be the costs of handling the five 'A' markets separately on an international basis; overlap, definition and arbitration difficulties between the work of product development and market development; and the psychological problems of

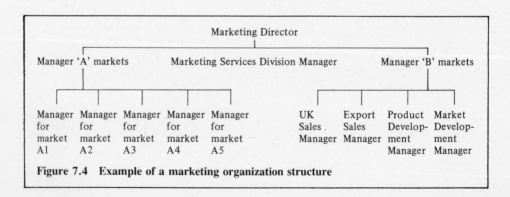

Figure 7.4   Example of a marketing organization structure

moving responsibility for newly developed markets from 'B' division to 'A' division. We postulated several other alternative structures which, while eliminating some of these latent difficulties, did not achieve the advantages of this recommended solution.

The key lessons from this structure are:

1 To plan the organization from the marketplace inwards;
2 To identify the key characteristics of the different market systems around which the organization can be structured;
3 As far as possible to keep planning and implementation (thus profit responsibility) together;
4 To focus particular resources on particular problems, or, in this case, future opportunities for growth;
5 To keep common only those functions which can be cost-effectively centralized;
6 To eliminate as far as possible potential interface problems;
7 To be prepared to consider alternative structures until the best available compromise between strengths and weaknesses can be selected.

These criteria at least can and should be applied in any organizational review.

CHECKLIST

1 Do we fully understand how the current structure evolved?

2 Have we defined all the tasks to be performed?

3 Have we considered more cost-effective ways of performing them?

4 Have we grouped the tasks of planning and implementation according to marketplace criteria?

5 Does the structure sufficiently reflect the particular opportunities and/or problems facing us?

6 Have we established staffing levels on the basis of workload analysis?

7 Is the marketing organization effectively integrated with other corporate activities, notably production and finance?

Chapter 8

Staffing the Structure

Creating a structure which reflects the needs of the marketplace and balances them with the corporate objectives and activities is only the first, although a very important, step in developing organizational effectiveness. However powerful the organization chart may look, it is the people it represents who will determine the success or otherwise of the structure. Most critical of all is the Marketing Director himself; for the quality of his leadership of the marketing team and of his contribution to the top management group must crucially affect the marketing activity in particular and corporate progress in general.

Peter Drucker identified five key practices that characterize effective senior executives.* Although his observations were made many years ago, his conclusions were so fundamental that they still seem totally valid; if anything, their significance has been heightened by the increasing complexity of business which can confuse even the most experienced senior manager. Drucker's five key factors are:

1 Effective executives know where their time goes. They work systematically at managing the little of their time that can be brought under their control.
2 Effective executives focus on outward contribution. They gear their efforts to results rather than to work.
3 Effective executives build on strengths – their own strengths, the strengths of their superiors, colleagues and subordinates, and on the strengths in the situation; that is, on what they can do.
4 Effective executives concentrate on the few major areas where superior performance will produce outstanding results. They force themselves to set priorities ... They know that they have no choice but to do first things first and second things not at all.

*Peter Drucker, *The Effective Executive*, Heinemann, 1967, Pan Books, 1970.

5   Effective executives finally make effective decisions.... They know that an effective decision is always a judgement based on 'dissenting opinions' rather than on 'consensus on the facts'.

Drucker was commenting on executives in general rather than Marketing Directors in particular. It is worth while therefore considering more specifically how these factors affect top marketing management. The first factor is the question of time management which concerns most Marketing Directors as they feel desperately short of 'thinking time' to consider future directions and activities. Unless positive action is taken, the situation is likely to worsen as marketing operations become increasingly international and as major customers demand higher-level negotiation. Both these circumstances are likely to involve the Marketing Director personally more and more and only part of the work can be delegated. This means that other duties may have to be shifted; the Marketing Director's span of control may well have to be reduced in order to free some of the time taken in management supervision to be used on these personal functions and still leave sufficient opportunity for thinking about the future. A good approach is for the Marketing Director to consider what he *must* do well rather than what he *can* do best and shed some or all those duties which are not essential. While such a process might sound self-evident it has to be conducted regularly because of the changing environment in which the Marketing Director operates.

The second factor is the focusing of attention on results rather than activities. Although obvious this requires strict self-discipline because of the difficulties of quantifying cause–effect relationships in marketing, particularly when a long time elapses between inputs and outputs. Furthermore, the important results are determined by many external as well as internal factors, and it is only too easy to focus more attention on the latter because they are more directly controllable than the former. This phenomenon has already been discussed in Chapter 6 in relation to planning systems which so easily become time-consuming ends in themselves. The Marketing Director should perhaps ponder this point in conjunction with the fourth factor, that of concentrating attention on the 'few major areas where superior performance will produce outstanding results'.

Because his personal time is the only resource that cannot be expanded, it must be concentrated on achieving a limited number of key priorities. Unless care is taken, it is only too easy to fall into the 80:20 trap where 80 per cent of the time is spent on activities which at best affect only 20 per cent of the results.

The third factor of building on strength emphasizes this point. The effective Marketing Director must ensure that both he and his whole team concentrate on the markets, products and people which can yield success and growth. Intensified promotion of a dying product or continuous counselling and retraining of incompetent personnel at best merely postpones the inevitable while absorbing resources of money and especially time which could be more productively used elsewhere.

Finally comes the key factor of effective decision making, which is often peculiarly difficult in the marketing area where not only can most of the decisions that have to be made today only be judged in the longer-term future, but also they depend upon the predicted reactions of people outside the company such as consumers, distributors and customers. Furthermore, facts on which the decisions can be based are often difficult and expensive to collect and are rapidly outdated. These complications should not cause perfection to become the enemy of the good; if we cannot be 100 per cent certain then we might as well guess. Drucker makes the points that decision making must be systematic; that 'getting the facts' in any case is impossible until it is known what facts are relevant; that it is more effective to hypothesize alternatives and test them while recognizing that, at top management level in particular, there are seldom any absolutely right, though there are many probably wrong decisions. Where the choice is clear the decision will usually have been taken lower down in the organization.

To run a successful marketing organization, the Marketing Director must organize his own time so that he can concentrate and decide on the few key result areas that can make a significant difference to corporate success. But he can only function if beneath him he has an effective team. This means ensuring first and foremost that the right people are in the right jobs and then that they are given appropriate training and development, that the work to be done is organized effectively, that commuications flow easily and that everybody involved is motivated to achieve the company's progress.

Key principles of staffing

Although it may be recognized that there are a few outstanding individuals who make particular and unique contributions and that therefore it may be worth while creating positions around their peculiar talents, if this is extended as a general principle it normally causes organizational chaos. This is because the following fundamental principles of effective staffing tend to be overlooked in the desire to accommodate personalities. Effective staffing should start by ensuring that:

1 The key results to be achieved by each job are specified.
2 The key taks that must be performed well are identified within each job.
3 Levels of responsibility are matched with levels of authority.
4 The relationships between the job and superior, subordinate and colleague functions are delineated so that management, information and communication systems can be clearly established.
5 The criteria by which performance in the job will be evaluated are specified.
6 The job is large enough to keep one person fully occupied but not so big that there is a danger that key tasks are not carried out thoroughly (i.e. there is a realistic workload).

Using these guidelines each job in the organization should be defined in writing; by studying such job descriptions together, gaps or duplications can be more easily identified. The problem with job descriptions in many organizations is that they tend to be too detailed about the activities to be carried out, rather than concentrating on the results to be achieved. This not only makes them too long to be used easily as working tools, but also limits their efectiveness as yardsticks for evaluating performance. Focusing the job description on the key result areas helps identify the essential tasks from which criteria of success can be more readily formulated. In some companies, such an approach has been institutionalized as 'management by objectives', but care needs still to be taken that in installing formal MBO systems, the medium does not become the message. In our experience MBO systems most frequently fail because they are allowed to become too detailed and too ritualized. More attention then tends to be paid to completing the forms according to the book than to ensuring that the tasks that affect success are identified, carried out and evaluated.

Only when the Marketing Director is satisfied that he has a complete set of descriptions which specify the key tasks and activities for each job in particular (and thus together the organization in general), should he consider the people needed. Admittedly such separation of the job to be done from the person to do it is psychologically much more difficult when appraising an existing organization than when staffing a new structure. But unless such discipline is maintained, there is a danger that the key task definition may be unduly influenced by the particular abilities of the current incumbent.

For example, where the sales manager gained his present position by having been the best salesman, it is only too easy to identify personal sales activity as being the key task of sales management and to overlook the equally and often more important factors of development and motivation of the whole sales team. This causes particular problems when the position becomes vacant for whatever reason; the tendency then is to replace the man rather than fill the job because the job has been in effect defined around the previous occupier. In these cases the organization drifts away from its objectives as fruitless attempts are made to duplicate personality profiles instead of reconsidering the results to be achieved, and the essential tasks to achieve them.

By starting with the results and the tasks, it is normally possible to define the kind of person that is likely to be successful. Such man or woman profiles provide the second step in a systematic staffing procedure. Care must be taken however to define such profiles within realistic limits of human ability and performance. In reading such profiles in companies, the impression we often gain is that the organization needs to be staffed with people of such intellect, character, education, experience and expertise that they would all be totally qualified for the highest levels of general management, if not sainthood!

In a similar way to stating the key tasks to be performed, the profile should identify the key attributes that are required, accepting that no one is perfectly rounded. With any set of strengths there will be weaknesses, but it is also worth identifying any weaknesses that cannot be afforded as they might cause failure. This analysis is particularly important when moving personnel from one position to what appears to be a broadly similar job. Failure to recognize the particular domestic pressures of international marketing has caused successful home market executives who have been moved into overseas locations to fail for personal reasons which did not affect their performance in the previous job.

The key to ensuring an effective marketing organization is to place people with the appropriate strengths in jobs where those strengths are necessary for the achievement of the required results even though it is likely that many will also possess weaknesses that have to be tolerated. Sometimes it is wise to consider a complementary staffing approach; if it is unrealistic to expect the complete range of strengths in one person, to cover any deficiencies by the careful staffing of closely related jobs. Thus in the sales management example quoted earlier, it may be decided that it is impractical to expect one person to possess the high level of personal selling skill and also the full range of development and motivational abilities. Thus the tasks may have to be divided between the sales manager, a deputy or regional manager subordinates, and staffed with persons who, with different strengths, together cover the full range required. It is for such reasons that some sophisticated fast-moving consumer goods companies have maintained both Marketing Director and Sales Director positions as they feel that the range of strengths required to fulfil both sets of tasks are unlikely to be found in one person, even though such a decision brings with it other organizational problems as discussed in the preceding chapter.

Placement and promotion

Running a marketing organization is of course a dynamic activity; key tasks change, jobs become vacant because of promotion, retirement or people leaving the company for a variety of reasons.

In filling vacant positions the existing job description and person profiles should be reconsidered to ensure that they are still valid. Most companies prefer to fill vacancies internally and this is usually preferable as it eliminates the induction process, there is first-hand evidence of the person's previous performance and it is generally motivational. Care needs to be taken that knowledge of the person being considered for promotion is properly used. It must be clearly understood that any candidates should be evaluated against the criteria for the future job, rather than be judged simply on the results in their present position. It is now almost a cliché that the best salesman seldom makes the best sales manager; the reasons why this is so are less widely understood. The key tasks and therefore the key strengths required for the two positions are usually very different. The successful salesman operates largely as an individual and requires a high level of skill in the personal persuasive communication process. The successful sales manager's task is to achieve results through others which requires skill in recruiting, selecting, planning, training, organizing, motivating and controlling his team. In addition, he will usually be involved in high-level selling, sometimes alone, more often with one or more of his sales force. Thus sales ability alone is a qualification for only one part of the required managerial range and even outstanding sales ability does not overcome, and may even exacerbate any deficiencies in the other key tasks. The newly promoted, highly successful salesman who lacks real managerial aptitude often tries to do the impossible of selling for his whole team, rather than enabling them to sell.

Similarly the marketing planning manager who has demonstrated a high level of skill in creating and implementing new product programmes, effective promotional campaigns, etc. may not be qualified to fulfil the Marketing Director position where ability to conceive long-term strategy, handle personally key accounts, or integrate the activities with other corporate functions may be the key tasks.

Judging how a person is likely to perform in a new position is of course much more difficult than assessing performance in the current job which is another reason why the latter tends to be overweighted. Nevertheless, the extra effort is always worth making for the resolution of any mistakes of appointment is always difficult, costly and time-consuming.

Recruiting and selecting external candidates

It is sometimes necessary, and often desirable in terms of broadening the corporate experience, to fill some positions from outside the company. Recruiting and selecting external candidates should follow the same principles as the promotion of internal staff, but even more care is needed to ensure that applicants thoroughly understand what is required of them and that the manager or director conducting the recruitment systematically obtains and verifies the appropriate information on each candidate. This means that whatever recruitment medium is used – advertising, registers, executive search – the information communicated about the job must be designed to attract relevant candidates. The number of applications is a poor criterion for judging recruitment success especially if the majority nowhere near match the requisite profile. In assessing candidates, we find that the best guide to how a person will perform in the future is an understanding of how he or she has performed in the past in every aspect of their life relevant to the position to be filled. This may extend beyond their work history into education, social or domestic aspects, not only where there is a direct overlap between these and the job to be done, but also because performance characteristics may have only been demonstrated in areas other than previous employment.

For example, in filling a management position there may be candidates who have not yet had direct management experience, but who seem to have relevant abilities. It is worth examining whether they have demonstrated any such talent in their other activities, e.g. seeking out managerial-type positions in school, university, local affairs, sports clubs, drama groups etc. Any data such as these are better than none at all even though they may seem distant from the commercial management role. It is the systematic collection and checking of all such information that is the basis of sound recruitment and selection procedures.

This means that all candidates should complete detailed application forms; the data provided should be verified and expanded (with prior permission of course) by telephone or in person with at least two referees, preferably previous employers; thorough interviews should be conducted covering all aspects in depth (which usually means at least 1½–2 hours each); shortlisted candidates should be interviewed at least twice, preferably by different people; and that even after all that, no appointment should be made unless there is a very high degree of confidence in the ultimate candidate.

Heavy stress is being laid on the recruitment and selection process because no marketing organization can be successful if it does not have the right people, which means persons with the essential capability in terms of personality characteristics and previous experience to bring the necessary strengths to the key results and tasks. Of course, people can be developed in terms of knowledge, skill and attitude. Our repeated experience and that of many others involved in management and staff recruitment is, however, that there is no commercially practical means of changing character or personality, especially in the mature age range from which the company normally recruits its marketing management or sales staff.

If this premise is accepted, the only practical approach (apart from continuously changing the jobs to fit the people, which has already been suggested as not a very effective way of operating) is to collect, verify and rigorously analyse as much data as possible about each apparently qualified candidate. We would always recommend that the collection process is conducted on carefully designed company forms; relying on even detailed curriculum vitae supplied by applicants can be dangerous as emphasis will obviously be laid on the successful elements of the past and more questionable areas may be rationalized, disguised or even omitted.

This is one of the key reasons for conducting telephone reference checks, again using a standard format to record the information; not only do they give the past superiors' opinions on performance (which may be very different from the applicant's self-rating) but also they often reveal errors of omission or commission in the data previously collected on the application form. In our experience a significant percentage of information is misrepresented by candidates. This ranges from minor modifications of, for example, job titles (e.g. Assistant to the Marketing Manager being listed as Assistant Marketing Manager, a small but perhaps vital change!) to major falsification. We have encountered several cases where periods of time spent in unsuccessful jobs, unemployed, or even in prison, have been omitted, perhaps understandably. The company has the need and the right to know the truth, however painful, if it is to make not only the correct judgement of the right person for the job but equally importantly, the right job for the person. In one case, we only discovered by detailed analysis that an apparently highly qualified candidate for a sales management position in an ethical pharmaceutical company had been convicted of impersonating a doctor. If he had been appointed, not only would the company's reputation have been obviously at risk, but also the continuing temptation to the man would perhaps have been an unfair burden on him.

The in-depth interviewing of candidates is the key stage in the recruitment and selection process. We recommend that interviews are conducted in a structured way by questioning candidates about their previous experiences starting from the present and working backwards. It will be noted that this order is the reverse of the normal application form. This gives a different perspective and is also another simple check on the veracity of the candidate; successful falsification would require not only lying consistently on both the application form and later at the interview, but also lying consistently in reverse sequence! By the end of the interview process, considerable data should have been collected about the candidate amplifying that already obtained from the application form and the telephone checks. It is worth considering at this stage whether there are any other processes that could be useful in providing a basis for judgement. Psychological, personality and even graphological tests are used by some companies to give another perspective on candidates. We have not found such measures of much practical benefit, largely because there is no proven correlation between their results and managerial capability. However, if any tests can be devised which simulate reality, they can be very helpful. For example in our own company one of the basic attributes that is needed is that every executive must be capable of making effective presentations to small groups of client management. We had great difficulty in evaluating candidates' presentational abilities from the normal process of interviewing, etc; we now therefore require each applicant, as an integral part of our selection procedure, to make a presentation to a group of our own management which helps us to evaluate his abilities and him to experience at least one essential aspect of the job.

Making the placement decision

The information collected must now be evaluated against the criteria for the job as defined in the person profile. While this should be done as systematically, objectively and completely as possible, the Marketing Director should not lose sight of the three key decision criteria in the welter of forms, data and others' opinions.

First, does this person possess the key strengths needed regardless of all his other talents and any weaknesses (as long as these are not a recipe for disaster)? If he lacks any of the key strengths, what is the nature of the deficiency? If it is knowledge, skill or attitude, then perhaps he can be trained. If it is a personality factor, such as intelligence, stability, immaturity, ability to relate with other people or lack of leadership, it is doubtful, however impressive his experience and qualifications, whether it can be overcome short of restructuring the job. The higher the management position to be filled, the more important relatively are the character aspects, because professional or technical expertise can usually be provided by subordinates.

Second, how well will this person relate with his subordinates (through whom he must achieve his results), his colleagues (with whom he must

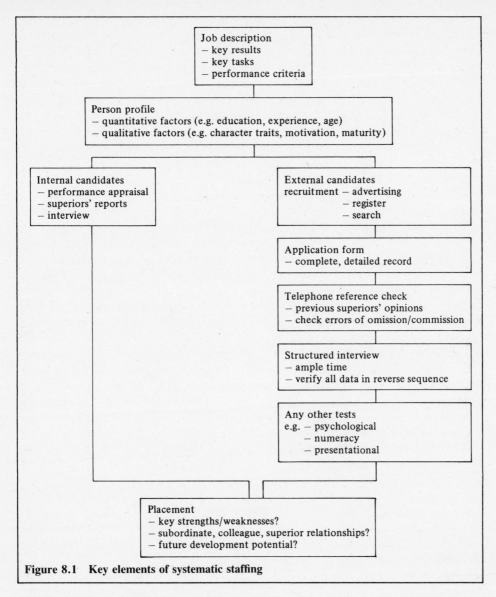

Figure 8.1   Key elements of systematic staffing

integrate his activities) and his superior (who must have the confidence to delegate to him and to allow him to function)? These questions of compatibility are often underrated although most Marketing Directors would accept that the harmonizing of the management team is vital to its effectiveness. This is not to say that a candidate's likeability is sufficient grounds for hiring; moreover care must be taken to avoid 'mirror image' selection which may merely duplicate existing strengths – and weaknesses. Harmony does not imply that everyone plays the same time on the same instrument. A successful orchestra needs different players playing different parts, but together and in time.

Third, does this person have potential beyond the job for which he or she is being recruited? The Marketing Director must ensure that tomorrow's management needs are considered as well as today's. This needs careful judgement. Too few people capable of promotion causes continuous problems of recruitment, too many might result in excessive turnover of ambitious managers and staff who feel their progress thwarted. To strike the appropriate balance requires some form of management succession planning. Starting from the longer-term objectives and strategies, the nature and scale of the future marketing organization, and thus the types and numbers of jobs sould be delineated. Each member of the current team should be assessed, against at least three basic criteria – is this person so barely competent that a change would be preferable, competent but incapable of greater responsibilities, or competent with potential for promotion? Even such a simple analysis should give some guidelines as to what percentage of people should be recruited with future potential at which levels. This can mean adopting a differential staffing approach, i.e. at any level whilst always recruiting people capable of the immediate tasks, selecting some, though not all, with a view to future promotion. In a marketing planning activity, for example, it can cause almost as many difficulties if all the product or brand managers are capable of immediate promotion as having none with further potential.

Effective staffing demands an understanding of the key results and activities of each job and the systematic assessment and placement of people in them who possess the key strengths needed (see Figure 8.1). Each individual must also be considered in relation to his role in the team and his potential for the future. Because marketing organizations are dynamic, the team must be capable of developing to meet future challenges whilst being stable, productive and satisfied in the current situation.

CHECKLIST

1 *Key characteristics of effective executives*

1.1 Do I effectively measure and control the use of my time?
1.2 Do I focus my attention on results rather than activities?
1.3 Have I built the organization on its strengths?
1.4 Do I identify and concentrate attention on the few key areas where significant results can be obtained?
1.5 Do I make effective decisions?

2 *Key principles of staffing*

2.1 Are all jobs clearly and concisely defined, with key results, key activities and evaluation criteria specified?
2.2 Have person profiles been constructed identifying the key strengths that must be possessed?
2.3 Have we considered complementary staffing in order to strengthen the team?
2.4 Do we base placement decisions on predicted capability in the job to be filled rather than on performance in the current position?
2.5 Do we have a systematic recruitment and selection procedure which collects and verifies all relevant information?

Chapter 9

Running an Effective Marketing Organization

Having the right structure and the right people are prerequisites for an effective marketing operation. However, the organization will only run successfully if the management and staff are developed, the work organized, good communications established and the whole team motivated. These are all continuous processes that the Marketing Director needs to monitor carefully.

Developing knowledge and skills

Management and staff training and development is now a well-accepted activity in most companies, although it is costly and time-consuming. It can be a powerful way of ensuring that the corporate personal assets yield increasing returns and growth.* Furthermore by ensuring that present management and staff are kept up-to-date and equipped to handle their changing key tasks and activities, external recruitment, which is so often triggered by the need to bring in new knowledge and skills, can be reduced. Because of the importance of building and maintaining an effective team, the Marketing Director should see training and development as an integral part of his responsibilties even though he may delegate some of the activity to others such as the personnel department or outside professional help. He should therefore understand at least the basic principles of the development process.

*The Centre for Interfirm Comparison's Study, *Management Policies and Practices and Business Performance*, 1977, showed that 'firms with formal management development programmes had much better overall performance scores than the majority.'

132

Successful management training is not a simple matter of sending a few people on a few courses. It should start with a detailed training needs analysis. First, the required knowledge, skill and attitudes should be identified from an analysis of the job description and person profile. Second, the present performance of the person in the job should be examined against these criteria. Third, the gaps between the desired and the actual levels should be specified and formulated into training objectives. These should describe what the person being trained should be able to do at the end of his training, the conditions within which he should be able to do it and the standards of performance that he should be able to achieve.

The training methods should then be considered in terms of their likely cost-effectiveness. The prime choices will be training on the job, in-company courses or external programmes. On-the-job training is a fundamental responsibility of every line manager and for many of the training needs, especially for new recruits, can be the appropriate method. However, care needs to be taken that such so-called 'sit by Nelly' techniques do match the identified needs, do not perpetuate outdated practices and are conducted by managers who themselves have had some training in training.

In-house courses, whether run by company personnel or consultants, have the advantages that part or all of the sales, marketing or management team can be developed together and that the programme can be based on the company's own particular circumstances. There has been a very significant and continuing swing from external to internal training over the last few years, as many organizations have concluded that outside programmes, while broadening the trainee through association with executives from similar positions in other companies, could not be specific enough to achieve their particular development goals.

Thus the trainee found great difficulty in applying what he had learnt on a general programme to the specifics of his own job, especially if his colleagues, and especially his superior, had not undergone similar training and therefore perhaps could not fully appreciate his changed knowledge, skill and attitude. The 're-entry problem', as it has become known, taxes the minds of all those concerned with management and staff development. The best approach we have found is to try to eliminate it rather than overcome it, by designing training programmes more closely within the context of the job. For example, in developing sales management in selection techniques, careful analysis soon reveals that while knowledge of the methods involved is necessary, what is vital is skill in asking questions and interpreting the answers. While knowledge can be inculcated by a variety of methods (books, films, lectures, learning packages), skills can only be developed by practise with constructive criticism and guidance. Although techniques such as role-playing interviews can develop the basic skills, by their nature they are at best only a simulation of reality. Therefore, we have designed and run a number of selection skill development programmes involving actual candidates for sales jobs as interviewees, with their permission, of course. The manager being trained conducts the interview as he would normally, the whole process being recorded on videotape for later tuition and analysis within the training programme. Similarly, we teach marketing planning skills using not simply traditional case studies, but the actual company situation so that by the end of the training programme, the managers have both learnt the knowledge and skills needed and also produced at least a well-advanced draft of their actual marketing plans.

This integration of management development with the actual job is a very powerful and cost-effective approach to training and obviously removes any 're-entry' difficulties. Although the contributions of on-the-job training or more general internal or external courses are not to be disparaged, such 'in-the-job' development concepts are likely to become more widely utilized especially in the search for improvements in training cost-effectiveness. Because of this need to improve development efficiency many organizations are now using learning packages ranging from simple programmed instruction manuals to sophisticated audio-visual programmes. Increasingly, companies are finding that it is worth producing tailored packages rather than relying on the general products available. Training packages are often the only practical solution where there are large numbers of people to be trained, especially when they are geographically spread, often internationally. For example, a multinational industrial corporation, recognizing a worldwide need to upgrade the performance of its distributor management and staff, commissioned us to develop a range of learning packages which could be easily adapted, translated and administered locally by non-professional trainers as this was the only practical and economic solution to the problem.

The training and development of management and staff is a powerful tool for increasing organizational effectiveness. In an increasingly dynamic and competitive world, the need for improved knowledge and skills becomes ever more important. The Marketing Director must accept the responsibility as head of the marketing team for arranging relevant and continuous development even though he may delegate its design and implementation to others. Unless he does, he will be left ultimately with no other way of equipping the organization with the necessary expertise than extensive external recruitment.

Oganizing the work

Running a cost-effective marketing organization demands that the work is carried out at the lowest possible level. It is often forgotten that the rationale for the delegation process is a financial one; the higher the level the greater the time and opportunity cost. Effective delegation confers other benefits too in terms of providing job satisfaction, development of the individual and greater freedom of top management time. However, our surveys of managerial attitudes often reveal at all levels in the organization a perception (usually justifiable) that work is either insufficiently or inefficiently delegated.

A review of the delegation processes throughout the structure should be conducted from time to time to ensure that all managers understand its nature and are delegating effectively. Delegation consists of three elements: delegation of responsibility which most directors and managers find relatively easy; delegation of authority (which most find difficult); and the maintenance of accountability, which makes the difference between delegation and abrogation. To delegate effectively demands that the delegator understands the economic rationale underlying the process and, most important of all, accepts that the tasks will often be performed differently from the way he would personally carry them out and sometimes with worse results.

Although poor results should not be complacently accepted, it should be recognized that it can be more productive to achieve less good results at a lower level if the higher-level time thus freed is employed effectively. The total results can therefore be greater than if no delegation is carried out. Allowing mistakes to be made is an inevitable part of the delegative process, but as long as mistakes are seen as development opportunities, they can be used to produce longer-term value.

With such concepts in mind, the delegator should ensure congruence between the responsibility and authority to be delegated. Regardless of what the job description might say, in practice no member of staff can in effect discharge more responsibility than the limits of his power. For if he is not allowed to take the relevant decisions or does not control the appropriate resources then he cannot in reality fulfil the associated responsibilities. This is a particular problem in those companies which want to believe they have delegated 'profit responsibility' to, for example, product or brand managers, despite the fact that such managers usually control very few of the key activities which affect profitability. If the sales force is ineffective, it is pointless attempting to pin responsibility for poor profits on the product manager. It is much more realistic to redefine his job within the limits of his power, and should such examples be widespread, even reconsider whether there are flaws in the company's organization which are preventing the proper linking of responsibility and authority.

The maintenance of accountability, i.e. the delegator himself accepting responsibility for ensuring that his subordinates discharge their duties effectively, is often the key to an effective delegative process. The delegator should define in advance the criteria by which his subordinates will be evaluated, what information he requires for such reviews, and how often assessments will be made. Otherwise the temptation is for the delegator constantly to check up on his staff as he fears things might be going wrong. This is usually perceived by the subordinate as interference which is very demotivational. Worst of all, the rationale for delegation is destroyed because the delegator is spending his time reviewing and often duplicating his staff's efforts. The construction of a more effective feedback mechanism for accountability at least reassures the delegator that he will discover soon enough if the work is being inefficiently carried out. Digging up plants every few minutes to make sure the roots are growing is a certain way of ensuring they don't!

For certain tasks the delegation of work to individuals may not be appropriate. There are activities which demand collective consideration and decision because they involve inputs from different functions (e.g. new product development) or a corporate view to be taken (e.g. company objectives). In such cases committees are usually formed to handle some or all of the work. The Marketing Director needs to review carefully such committees within his own organization to ensure they have not been caused by faulty structure or that they are not self-perpetuating or reproducing. Each committee's objectives should be clearly specified and checked to make certain that the work could not be handled by one individual, that each is run effectively, i.e. with agendas and working papers circulated in advance under strong chairmanship which allows everybody to make a contribution, prevents lengthy circular discussion, summarizes and reaches decisions which are then minuted and followed up to ensure implementation.

Committees, meetings, working groups and the like are an inevitable and essential feature of commercial life; they provide forums for discussion resulting in ideas, directions and decisions which it is unlikely one individual would ever develop. The problem of committees is in their abuse and they should be restricted to those circumstances where several heads are indubitably better than one to exploit opportunities or resolve problems; otherwise they prevent organizational effectiveness if only because they absorb vast quantities of the scarcest resource of all, management time.

Establishing effective communications

Virtually every enterprise we work with complains of 'communication problems', often thought to be caused by not having enough information. Significantly, these difficulties do not seem to be eased and are often exacerbated by the vast growth of available data within marketing organizations. The 'information explosion' as it has been called is a result of the rapid development of management information systems which are increasingly computer-based. However, it appears that the corporate capacity to collect and process data has in many cases far outstripped management's ability to use it. We are often forced to conclude that the 'communication problem' is in fact being tackled from the wrong end. There is no point producing more data if existing information is not being productively used.

Effective communication in the marketing organization must start with an analysis of who needs to know what for what purposes, how often and how accurately. An organization structure can be described as a human decision-making system. The decisions vary in magnitude from changes in corporate objectives or strategies to judging which orders should be processed first in the sales office. But every decision needs to be based on information if it is to be taken systematically and objectively. However, the data requirement is impossible to specify unless the nature of the decision is understood and therefore what facts will be relevant. The kind of data required from the marketplace, for example, to make new product development decisions is different from the market information for distribution or promotional judgements. What people buy, where they buy and how they buy are three quite different though interrelated questions. Thus calling for 'all there is to know about the market' is not precise enough a research brief; the terms of reference should be specified from the probable decisions to be taken, not from what is likely to be available.

Because of a lack of this kind of approach to specifying data requirements, many marketing organizations do not receive the data they need from their own internal information systems, especially financial data which tend to be a by-product of the basic accounting mechanisms of the company. Thus it is usually difficult to identify true revenue, costs and profits by customer which can be vital, particularly for key account negotiation judgements because such decisions were not considered in the construction of the system.

Similarly, data broken down by industry, market segment or distribution network are often not available though many judgements must be made on which segments or channels to choose and how to operate within them.

For example, in one industrial company where urgent decisions were needed on which end-user markets to select for concentration, we found the only sales data available were broken down by product and as the same products were sold to different end-users, it was difficult to identify the relative sizes and trends of the various markets served.

The analysis of what decisions have to be taken also helps specify who needs to know what if the key results and activities have been properly defined. However, there seems to be a misconception in some organizations that virtually everybody needs to know everything. All executives receive copies of all management data, most on a 'for information only' basis. A moment's reflection suggests that this is a meaningless phrase. If information cannot be used by the recipient for decision making, either directly or indirectly, there seems little point communicating it. Such widespread circulation of vast amounts of data tends to inhibit communication as frustrating amounts of time are spent wading through piles of paper with no productive result. This is particularly true in those organizations which have given too little thought to how often data should be collected, analysed and circulated. In one company, sales data are made available on a daily basis at great expense. This gives the impression of detailed control over the marketing activities. In fact marketing and sales management tends to disregard daily fluctuations as so many are random and make any decisions on weekly figures at least.

The need for accuracy of information is as often overrated as the need for frequency. The degree of accuracy required can often be assessed by considering what effect inaccuracy will have on the decision to be taken. For example, if it is being decided whether or not to enter a new market and it is thought that its size is £X million, it should be considered what level of inaccuracy would be significant before commissioning any research. If the market would still be of interest even though it may be £X million plus or minus 10 per cent, there is little point in spending money establishing a more precise figure.

Exactitude in any case is a myth for many types of marketing information. Although the computer prints out figures perfectly to many decimal places if so required, it must never be forgotten that its output can only be as accurate as its input. Furthermore, accuracy is a function of time as well as cost. It is often better for decision making to have fewer accurate data sooner than more accurate data later. If management accounting information (e.g. results v. budget) comes too late after the end of the period, vital time for corrective action may well be lost that may have been saved by earlier, though less precise estimates.

The basis of an effective communication system is the provision of the right data to the right people at the right time to enable them to make the best possible decisions to achieve their key results. But effective communication between the members of the marketing organization and between it and the other functions of the company can only be achieved by a recognition of the human problems of communication. Every person has his own particular set of psychological filters through which he transmits and receives communication and which modify the messages. To communicate effectively demands therefore that the message is transmitted in such a way that it can be received correctly through the filters of the recipient. While most marketing executives accept and practise this concept in external communications – advertising, promotion, selling – and recognize that understanding the needs of the receiver is the essential first step to successful persuasive communication, all too often the lesson is not applied within the organization. The failure of the superior to perceive and understand the needs and motivations of his subordinates, and vice versa, causes breakdown in vertical communication. Sales management feeling that the marketing planning department does not comprehend their problems, and vice versa, causes problems in horizontal communication. Such barriers to effective communication can only be overcome by improving the ability of all concerned to perceive more clearly the receiver's viewpoint. This can be done by increasing awareness and knowledge of others' tasks and problems through training, job rotation and constant highlighting of the situation in discussions and meetings. Good communications does not mean that everybody will always be in agreement but at least disagreements will not be based on failure to understand the viewpoint of others.

A case history that summarizes this whole approach to improving communication effectiveness is that of a large industrial company where there were serious communication difficulties between the marketing and the finance functions. The marketing and sales managers complained that they did not get the right information quickly enough on which to base, for example, pricing decisions. They felt that the finance staff did not understand or care about the problem they had with customers, but were only concerned about their own accountancy activities. On the other hand the finance staff felt that the marketing team demanded too much information too quickly which disrupted their routines and then when they had provided, for example, detailed costings, ignored them and set prices which bore no relationship to them.

The basis for improving communication between the two functions was laid by running a series of training programmes attended by both marketing and financial management. The objective was to explain and discuss the nature of marketing to the finance members and the nature of finance to the marketing executives. The various approaches to pricing decisions, for example, were considered and the relationship between marketing and financial inputs demonstrated. It became clear that marketing did not need the amount of detail finance were providing; in fact most of the data required could be extracted very easily and quickly from existing sources. Because of the lack of understanding of finance, the wrong questions had been posed by marketing. Because of this and insufficient marketing understanding, the finance staff not surprisingly had provided the wrong answers and had not felt confident enough to query the reasons for the requests.

The development of better understanding led to an increasing mutual respect for and trust in each others' abilities, which is essential for effective communication. Both sides began to reveal and modify their prejudices which had been founded on ignorance. New communication systems and flows were developed and more regular contact established. For example, detailed profitability information was made available regularly to marketing. It had always existed but marketing had never asked for it because they feared the finance reaction to more requests for information. Finance had never provided it because they feared marketing would not understand it and might misuse it.

Of course, marketing and finance still disagree from time to time but at least they now understand why they disagree. The marketing decision-making process has certainly been improved by better financial inputs and awareness and the two functions now work together more productively.

Motivating the marketing team

For the marketing team to be fully effective, it must not only be competent to carry out its activities; it must be motivated to do so. As every individual is different, so each is influenced by different motivations. The key role the Marketing Director must play is to lead the team consisting of such different individuals towards common objectives. He must direct his immediate subordinate managers so that they are motivated not only to employ their best abilities in their work, but also to motivate and lead their own staff.

Successful leadership starts with a full understanding of the needs of the individuals and satisfying those needs so that the staff are motivated to achieve the corporate aims. Obviously one basic need is for money which must be satisfied by a well constructed remuneration system which recognizes the marketplace values of the jobs in the organization and the quality of the individual's performance. However, while a poor pay system demotivates, it would be unwise to believe that a good salary and/or incentive scheme will provide positive and continuous motivation. In practice the satisfaction of financial needs does not act as a positive motivational influence.

The most powerful motivations are to be found in the way in which the job is constructed and managed. Most people work most effectively when they are certain what is to be achieved, they know how their achievement will be measured, their achievement is recognized, they feel part of the team, and they are given the opportunity to improve their performance and position in the future.

The goal-setting process is the first stage in providing a motivational environment. Wherever possible, goals, objectives and targets should be set in consultation so that the person concerned feels that he is making not only a contribution, but also a commitment to the decision. Goals should be set as far as possible in specific and quantified terms and with agreed time periods for achievement. This then provides a strong sense of direction and urgency.

The criteria by which progress towards the goals will be evaluated should also be made clear and results fed back regularly so that the person can measure his progress. Successful achievement should be praised, poor performance constructively criticized. This point comes out very strongly in surveys of what executives regard as the key qualities of good management. In reply to the question 'what were the outstanding features of the best manager you ever worked for?', a common response is that he gave both sincere praise and criticism whenever it was due.

Feeling part of the team is also very important to many people at all levels in the marketing organization. They want to work with others, for others and in many cases have others working for them. It is useful to view the organization as a series of interlocking teams with each individual a part of one or more. Thus the Marketing Director is a member of the top management team and the leader of the senior marketing team. The sales manager is a member of the senior marketing team and a leader of the sales team. The need to belong to a group is very basic and if frustrated causes severe demotivation. The team can achieve more than can each individual, it is a place for sharing success (and failure) and it gives security.

Most people want to feel they are progressing in their jobs, not simply repeating past performances. Efforts should be made to ensure that each job is continuously challenging by increasing its goals, broadening its responsibilities and enlarging its tasks. Job enrichment, as it has been termed, can provide a very positive and continuous motivation as can developing the person in the job. As well as its obvious learning benefits, training provides a powerful incentive as can be seen on any management development programme where executives often work harder and longer of their own volition and without any direct reward than they do in the office.

For many people, progress means promotion, but not all who want to move up are capable of higher managerial positions. Judging people on their capabilities for the next job, rather than simply on their performance in the current one has already been suggested as the best approach. But it can be demotivational for the outstanding performer at one level to be told this does not necessarily qualify him for the next, even when carefully explained. This is a particular problem in sales forces where highly successful salesmen may feel limited if they cannot progress. Some companies have dealt with this by creating a hierarchy within the sales function so that the successful salesman who lacks managerial capability can become progressively, senior salesman, account executive, key account manager, etc., shouldering bigger sales responsibilities with increasingly important customers and having his progress recognized by higher status and remuneration.

The ability to motivate and lead his team is at the very heart of the Marketing Director's task of running an effective organization. He must provide for his managers and ensure that they provide for their staff the key qualities that motivate people to work productively. From our studies, those that are rated most highly are decisiveness, willingness to praise and criticize, consistent fairness, acceptance of ultimate responsibility for the team (especially when things go wrong), professional capability, willingness to work at least as hard as his subordinates and ability to communicate and delegate.

Conclusion

The effective management of the marketing organization demands a synthesis of a number of highly complex processes: identifying the tasks to be performed; finding people capable of performing them, both individually and as a team; ensuring that they are equipped with requisite knowledge and skills; organizing the work to be done; establishing effective communications and motivating the team. (Every process is worthy of a book on its own; not surprisingly there are numerous texts on each.) Failure in any one area can cause a dramatic decrease in total effectiveness.

This chapter has highlighted some of the factors which we have found essential for the efficient running of the organization. Once the basic process is established, the Marketing Director's role should become analogous to that of a preventive maintenance engineer. By continuously monitoring the whole system, he should aim to avoid potential problems by putting his weight behind key recruitment decisions before the vacancy becomes urgent, freeing communication blockages before too many people leave and most important of all, keeping the organization focused on the results to be achieved in the marketplace rather than on internal activities. The smoothly running organization should be like an efficient factory, carrying out its work calmly without drama, panics and confusion. Endless urgent meetings, executives regularly working late into the night, the grapevine working better than the company communications systems, are all signs of an ineffectively run organization which may break down, only to be replaced by yet another new structure which rapidly becomes as inefficient as its predecessor.

The Marketing Director must also take prime responsibility for the interface with the other functions of the company. The tone of this will be set by his relationships with his board colleagues and should be continued at all levels down the structure. Perhaps above all, the Marketing Director should remember that he is usually the only professional persuasive communicator in the board room and therefore must take major responsibility for the establishment of good communications with the rest of the company.

CHECKLIST

1   *Developing knowledge and skills*

1.1   Do we conduct systematic training needs analyses?
1.2   Do we fit the training to the individuals precisely enough?
1.3   Do we relate training closely enough to the job?
1.4   Have we explored all the training methods available?
1.5   Is our training and development programme sufficient to equip the marketing team for the future?

2   *Organizing the work*

2.1   Are our delegation processes effective and perceived to be so?
2.2   Have we ensured that responsibility and authority are delegated together?
2.3   Have we constructed systems for maintaining accountability?
2.4   Have we reviewed all our meetings to ensure that they are necessary?
2.5   Are our meetings conducted effectively?

3   *Establishing effective communications*

3.1   Have we clearly defined our marketing management information needs?
3.2   Have we established systems which will provide the relevant data to the right person quickly and accurately enough?
3.3   Does communication flow smoothly up and down the marketing organization?
3.4   Does it flow smoothly across the marketing organization?
3.5   Does the marketing organization have effective communication with the other company functions?

4   *Motivating the marketing team*

4.1   Have we identified the prime motivational needs of our management and staff?
4.2   Have we a sound remuneration system?
4.3   Do our people feel consulted, involved and committed both individually and as part of the team?
4.4   Do we provide enough opportunities for growth?
4.5   Are we providing motivationally effective management?

Chapter 10

Evaluating and Controlling the Marketing Activity

The central task of the Marketing Director, as of any other manager, is to produce results. Once the objectives have been set, the strategies formulated, the marketing plans laid and their implementation started, the Marketing Director must ensure that there is a control process which can monitor performance and progress and identify any areas where corrective action is needed. The key to the construction of an effective evaluation procedure is the definition of the criteria against which actual performance can be assessed. Comparison of such standards and actual results will produce in some cases variances which signal the need for corrective action in order to put the company back on course towards the achievement of its goals.

Setting standards for evaluating marketing performance

The yardsticks for performance should be capable of being defined from the objectives and plans of the company, if these have been properly formulated. A good test of the objectives and plans is to decide during their construction how their achievement will be measured. This encourages the setting of specific goals and actions, where possible quantified, timed and costed. A good approach to the definition of such criteria is to consider two basic questions: what will constitute 'success' in this area?, and what factors will affect the achievement of that 'success'? The first question forces specification of the level of the desired *effects*, the second the identification of the prime *causes*. Although it is the achievement of results (profit, sales, market share, etc.) that is the goal of the marketing activity, it is only on the

143

basis of an understanding of their causes, both external and internal, that appropriate corrective action can be planned. Furthermore, it is only the causes that can be directly influenced by any corrective action. Thus a monitoring procedure which only measures results does not in fact constitute an effective control system; to know that sales are below target is of little value unless why they are below target is also known. Yardsticks by which the factors affecting success can be evaluated should therefore be specified. Such diagnostic criteria should be set for both external factors (the market, the distributive system, competitive activity) and internal factors (products, price, promotion), even though it is difficult to identify the full complexities of the cause–effect relationships in marketing.

As has already been suggested, answering the question of 'what constitutes success?' i.e. specifying the desired results, is usually relatively easy if the objective setting and planning process has been thorough. There are three categories of performance for which measurement criteria should be set: market performance, distributive performance and corporate performance.

Market performance is often defined simply in terms of market share, but it is prudent to refine and expand such traditional criteria. First, the standards by which the market itself is defined should be considered, since the needs to be satisfied and particularly the means of satisfaction can and do change. For example, an office stencil duplicator manufacturer who traditionally measured his market performance in terms of his share of total duplicator sales had to change his definition of the market to one encompassing all types of office copying in order to establish a realistic measurement of his own performance. The development of other means of supplying the same needs, e.g. photocopiers, small printing machines, word processors, meant that a market at one time totally supplied by duplicators could no longer be accurately specified by that one product.

Second, even where the market is correctly defined, percentage share criteria should reflect how much of the total market is available. In many companies there are significant constraints of geographical coverage or distributive patterns which mean that the available market is very different from the total market. For example in the tyre industry where many of the distributors are owned by manufacturers, the total market in reality is not available to any of them. Thus share criteria are only realistic when subdivided into share in own outlets, share in competitive outlets and share in independent outlets.

Third, some companies prefer to use criteria of market position, often because accurate market share data are not available. They may specify, for example, that their desired standard is to be perceived as one of the top three suppliers. This is seen as important in one medical equipment company, particularly in overseas markets, where unless a supplier is of a certain size and reputation, he is unlikely even to be invited to tender for large government contracts. Of course, being a major supplier and being perceived as one need not be synonymous, and the criteria have to be defined for assessing both situations. Similarly, many firms who use market share criteria for the quantitative measurement of performance also develop yardsticks for assessing the perception of their company image, i.e. their qualitative performance.

Distributive performance criteria are traditionally defined in many companies in terms of how many outlets stock and sell their products as a percentage of the total number of outlets available. With the growing polarization in many trades with the large distributors becoming increasingly larger, such crude standards must be refined to reflect this. One of our Spanish clients in the perishable food industry was satisfied that a very high percentage of shops stocked his product. However, because the company had not penetrated very effectively into the rapidly growing supermarket sector of the trade, the distribution achievement in terms of value was far less and declining dangerously fast. This had not been perceived by the marketing team who had assumed that their 80 per cent distribution level by numbers of outlets implied a similar level as it had done in the past when the shops were more similar in size. Because of the importance of distribution to many companies, more sophisticated criteria need to be developed to monitor and control this aspect of marketing activity. Such standards can cover the percentage of business that should be done with each network or even major outlet and on what terms so that the Marketing Director can check that the appropriate balance is maintained. Some examples of this kind of approach were described in Chapter 3.

Corporate performance standards are usually embodied in the targets and budgets of the firm. Normally these will cover profit and profitability, sales by volume and value broken down by product group and/or market segment, and all the various cost elements of the marketing activity. Such criteria can often be made even more useful by being expressed in ratio terms; some companies use the management ratio hierarchy approach described in Chapter 3 and set standards for each ratio. Other firms have evolved yardsticks to assess other causal relationships such as sales cost:sales, advertising:sales, equipment sales:spare part sales, orders:calls, etc. Diagnostic criteria such as these which help evaluate the factors that affect the overall results of the company are particularly valuable to the Marketing Director as they can represent an early warning system giving time for corrective action.

For example, in one computer company where sales were measured simply against sales targets, it was noted that the business exhibited a two-year cyclical pattern. Analysis showed that this was because the average lead time between initial contact and final purchasing decision was likewise about two years; the sales force, which was the major marketing tool, made active prospecting efforts in the first year of the cycle, but gained few orders. In the second year they concentrated on surveys and clinching orders based on the previous year's prospecting, and sales increased. The year after, because of the lack of prospecting the previous year, sales declined as the initial stages of the sales process had to be recommenced. The situation was alleviated by setting standards not only for actual sales, but also for the other key stages in the sales process, e.g. prospecting, conducting feasibility studies and full surveys, all of which had to be achieved each year, thus creating a more balanced sales activity and a more even flow of orders.

Identifying the areas of the business where criteria should be established and deciding the format of such standards is the first step in establishing an effective marketing control system. It has been suggested that there are three broad areas where yardsticks are needed – the market, the distributive network and the company itself – and some criteria have been discussed. As each company is different, the Marketing Director should think through his particular circumstances and try to identify what Drucker has called the key transactions in the business.

In the marketing of fast-moving consumer goods these key transactions will include advertising:sales ratios relative to competition and the levels of distribution and display. In industrial capital equipment, other factors such as enquiry levels, invitations to tender, degree of customer contact and confidence are likely to be more important. In the hotel industry the room occupancy rate is a vital standard of success. All these examples share the common characteristic that the achievement of high levels of performance gives a sound basis for corporate success whereas low levels almost certainly mean failure. Of course, a hotel markets other services than overnight accommodation such as restaurants, bars, conference facilities etc., but on their own these can seldom replace loss of occupancy revenue and profits, whereas conversely high occupancy tends to have a positive effect on the sales of all other hotel services.

Ideally the Marketing Director should try to identify the sequence of key transactions which ultimately create the majority of sales and profits and establish criteria for each. Then by monitoring performance in the early stages of the sequence, there is time to take corrective action should variances begin to occur. In the computer company mentioned earlier, it was possible not only to identify the sequence of contacts made, feasibility study, survey and order, but also to quantify the relationship between them. For every order gained, on average three surveys had been submitted on which decisions had been made. For every three 'decisioned' surveys, five surveys had been conducted. For every five surveys, twenty short feasibility studies had been made to check whether a survey might be worthwhile. To produce twenty companies worthy of feasibility study required about one hundred contacts. Thus knowing the ratios of 1:3:5:20:100, the Marketing Director could monitor each phase of the marketing cycle and from evaluation of the earlier stages of contact and feasibility study predict the likely outcome and when necessary take corrective action in time to increase prospecting effort if sales were forecast to fall below target. Similarly a build-up of used car stocks in the dealer network alerts the motor manufacturer of future problems of selling new cars as ultimately the dealers will not have sufficient finance or space to stock nor perhaps the motivation to buy and sell them until they have cleared the excess of used vehicles.

Having defined the key areas of results and causes (and their sequence) for which criteria should be defined, the Marketing Director has then to set the appropriate levels for each. Unfortunately there are no formulae and relatively few general guidelines. There is no standard ratio for sales cost:sales or for advertising:sales which can be applied to all companies. However, research can sometimes demonstrate some basic relationships. For example, in the food industry brand leaders tend to maintain their position only if their share of total promotional expenditure is higher than their market share. In practice, each company has to make its own judgements based on past performance, other divisions' experiences or similar companies' achievements where these are obtainable. These can then be refined through analysis and in the light of the future plans of the company. To continue the computer company example, having identified the relationships between the various selling stages, the fact that gave most cause for concern was that two out of every five surveys submitted never came to a decision either for the company or its competitors. Conducting surveys is a very expensive process and the fact that 40 per cent were wasted warranted deeper investigation. This showed that although there were some cases of genuine changes of circumstances between the commissioning and completion of surveys (e.g. change of policy or finance availability) there were also a number of occasions where either the survey should never have been started as there was no chance of the prospective customer purchasing, or where there had been a lack of sales follow-through to persuade the prospective client to reach a decision. The computer company concluded that it was worth a great deal of effort to try to change the ratio from 5:3 to 4:3 by eliminating those surveys that should never have been conducted anyway. If such a revised standard of performance could be achieved, it would save not only considerable time and money, but also, without any other change in the relationships, 20 per cent of the feasibility studies and the prospecting, thus allowing further time for productive selling.

Comparing actual performance against standards

To exercise control, data about actual performance must be collected and assessed against the pre-set criteria. This implies a marketing management information geared to these yardsticks. All too often, however, as suggested in the previous chapter, the data available are determined by the requirements of finance or production and in many companies marketing has still to make do with the outputs of such corporate information procedures.

For many organizations this means that the creation of an effective marketing data collection system for the purposes of control has to start from first principles. What areas are we trying to measure? What criteria of evaluation will be used? How often do we need to compare actuals against standards? How many of the necessary data are available from the existing information systems? What new data collection and/or analysis procedures are needed?

For example, a major bank asked us to help develop a promotional programme aimed at increasing its business and profitability by encouraging good customers to use more of the bank's services. This involved being able to identify in each branch who were the good customers, what their needs were, and the likely business and profits to be generated by increasing sales of various services such as trustee help and insurance. Thus targets could be set with which the promotion campaign could be directed and evaluated. We found that the traditional information systems could produce a great number of facts about the bad customers (i.e. poor credit risks), but little or no data were available about the good clients (i.e. those who used the bank's facilities and paid for them on time). Even in the corporate sector there were few or no commercial data available about the business customers who had been identified as a prime target. Furthermore, there was no information on the profitability of the various bank services or indeed on each branch as a whole. Thus, in order to develop, run and assess the marketing programme which was very important to the bank's growth objectives, a completely new data base had to be constructed. It took on average three weeks per branch to collect and analyse the requisite information to enable the promotion to be effectively implemented and evaluated, a small investment of time relative to the significance of the campaign and a vital base for future planning and control. In this particular case, the information system installed was manual, but capable of being at least partially computerized when appropriate.

The development of computer technology and techniques means that many companies' marketing activities can now consider establishing their own information system geared to their own needs of measuring what is important, rather than continuing as in the past with evaluating only those factors on which data are available, almost coincidentally from other corporate systems. In a recent survey we conducted into the use of computers in marketing, more than half the Marketing Directors responding felt that the data processing service they were receiving currently from their own D.P. functions was unsatisfactory, largely because it was not geared specifically to their needs as it was based on standard financial reporting. Perhaps not surprisingly, three-quarters of the respondents hoped to have their own mini-computer or on-line facilities within the next three years now that the cost of such installations makes them viable even on a departmental basis.

As this increased computing power becomes available to the Marketing Director, he must try to avoid the common mistake of using the computer to produce even greater quantities of data. This problem can be averted by defining the information collection requirements from the criteria against which actual results will be ultimately compared. Furthermore, by entering such standards into the computer, it can be programmed to highlight the variances, thus producing a basis for 'management by exception'. This makes for a much more effective use of scarce management time by concentrating on variances from plan rather than reviewing continuously the total performance only to conclude that most activities need no corrective action.

From time to time, the ongoing information collection processes may need supplementing because a number of the criteria set may not be capable of internal evaluation, e.g. corporate image, advertising effectiveness, distribution levels. Regular research should be planned to collect the necessary data to enable an evaluation to be made of performance in such areas.

Evaluating and controlling management and staff performance

The Marketing Director needs to measure not only the performance of the marketing activities of the firm, but also the performance of the personnel, particularly as this will largely determine the achievement or otherwise of the marketing goals. A concept of control similar to that outlined above can be applied to human assessment based on answering such key questions as:

1   What constitutes success in this job?
2   What are the key factors that will affect success?
3   What are the key result areas and tasks to be performed?
4   What is their sequence and relationship?

Having developed a framework of criteria, they should be quantified or if they are qualitative, levels of performance should be specified by examining past levels of performance by the job-holder and others in similar positions and considering how the achievement might be improved in the future by changing priorities, providing more resources, developing knowledge and skills, etc.

Each person should be regularly appraised against the standards for the job and guided on how to improve performance. If such appraisals are to be effective they should concentrate on areas of improvement which are possible, i.e. techniques, skills, attitudes, not on elements of character or personality, as research has consistently shown that such traits are usually incapable of change. Critical appraisal of personality faults often causes performance to decline as the person concerned is made uncomfortably aware of his or her personality deficiencies for the job in question and yet is unable to correct them.

Performance appraisals should be conducted on at least an annual basis and preferably six month or quarterly. They should not take place at the same time as salary assessment, as there is often an overwhelming temptation to make the appraisal conclusions justify the decision on remuneration level which may be influenced by many factors other than the person's previous three months' performance.

Such a 'management by objectives' approach has proved to be very effective in a large number of companies, particularly when it is kept simple and focused on the main issues. Furthermore it provides an important input into the training needs analysis which should precede the construction and running of the management development programme.

Taking corrective action

The main purpose of any control system is to monitor performance against plan and where variances occur take corrective action. To do this, any variance must be analysed by first checking that the standards are still appropriate. Because the plans from which the criteria are derived often cover a long period, usually at least a year, some companies have a regular review process during the year which can lead to a reforecast or some rebudgeting to reflect better the changed reality. Obviously in such cases the criteria for performance evaluation must be modified too. The danger of such systems is that unless great care is exercised, the fact that regular changes are allowable reduces the original management commitment and motivation to the planning process. Nevertheless, whether such change is inherent in the planning system or not, it is wise, before taking action, to reflect on whether the criteria which produce the variances are still totally valid. In an increasingly volatile world, the appropriate action may be to modify the plan and thus the standards for evaluation.

Second, the actual data should be checked to ensure their comparability with the pre-set standards, and particularly to verify that any variance is significant and, if left unchecked, would form an unfavourable trend. It is possible for variances to occur for random reasons. For example, in comparing monthly data against targets, remember that the number of working days per month can vary according to the number of weekends, public holidays etc., by about 10 per cent. Such factors, plus coincidental timing of holidays, competitive activity, product shortage, etc. can all cause variances which do not indicate a need for corrective action. Some companies handle these situations by establishing variance limits in advance, similar to the concept of engineering tolerances; others use simple statistical techniques such as cumulative totals, averages, or moving annual totals to smooth out random fluctuations.

Assuming the variance is significant, the third step is to attempt to establish its causes. The three basic categories of cause are marketplace change (consumers, distributors etc.), competitive change (in products, prices or promotion), or internal change (in products, prices, promotion and personnel performances).

Fourth, corrective action can be planned when the cause or causes have been identified or at least hypothesized. New criteria should be set, the action programmed, timed and costed and careful evaluation made of the effectiveness of its implementation. This process is particularly important where management is not certain of the reasons for variance and some experimentation is necessary to establish the causes. Sadly, in too many companies, once a cause has been decided upon as the most plausible, action is taken across the board, thus destroying the ability to hold a control group to demonstrate whether or not the real causes have been identified.

As an example of this experimentation, a mail order company identified a significant variance against its criterion of sales per agent. A number of explanations were suggested – e.g. that the number of customers per agent was declining, the sales level of each was declining, the agents were buying simply for themselves and their immediate families, rather than acting as intended as sales channels. It was further postulated that if the agents were better motivated by incentives and better communications, they would be likely to sell more. However, the costs of such an exercise could only be justified if sales revenues above a certain level were generated.

Rather than establish a general promotional scheme, it was decided to run a controlled experiment not only to test, but also to quantify the cost:revenue relationships between agent motivation and sales generated. Two large groups of agents were selected on a matched basis as far as was possible. Sales targets were set for the first group and a communication and promotion programme established which, if it caused the targets to be met, would result in an overall profit increase. The second group continued to be handled as before. The test was run over a six-month period and the results compared against the control group. As so often happens, the control group sales changed due to the general situation and declined by about 5 per cent; however the test group increased by 5.6 per cent. The only difference between the two groups was the promotion and communication programme and thus the cause-effect relationships could be established and quantified. Of course, if would be going too far to suggest a national campaign would guarantee the same results as other variables could come into play, but certainly a careful, measured extension of the promotion programme would be likely to produce beneficial effects.

Conclusion

Evaluating and controlling the marketing activity is always difficult as marketing, if a science at all, is a social, not a physical science. Many of the causal relationships involved are complex and not totally understood; it is impossible to control all the variables involved, and some of the elements can only be described qualitatively (e.g. the creativity of advertising). Nevertheless, the Marketing Director cannot afford either to make perfection the enemy of the good (and thus as perfect control is impossible, control nothing) or merely to evaluate what is measurable, rather than what is important.

The key to an effective evaluation and control procedure is the identification of the vital factors in the total marketing activity that must be assessed and the establishment of criteria for their measurement. Given a framework of standards which cover these important elements, it is relatively easy to define the actual data requirement and thus the management information system. Variance production and analysis is more difficult, particularly the correct specification of causal factors, but experiment and research do offer some methods for testing hypotheses with the chance at least of adding to the corporate knowledge of how marketing actually works. Notwithstanding the natural tendency of management towards urgent action, a little reflection and testing might cause the right things to be done albeit more slowly. As was said ruefully about a major international company which has since run into serious difficulties, the management's first reaction to an overseas problem was to leap on an aeroplance – its second was to think about it!

Finally, it should always be remembered that planning and control are like opposite sides of the same coin. There is little point in planning unless the results are evaluated and one of the major purposes of such evaluation is to improve future planning.

CHECKLIST

1 Have we defined the key areas of marketing activity that need to be evaluated?
2 Have we defined what is 'success' in each area?
3 Have we identified the factors that will affect success in each area?
4 Have we established appropriate criteria for evaluating market-place, distributive and corporate performance?
5 Do we have a clear concept of the sequence of causal factors?
6 Does our management information system provide appropriate data to compare against the key criteria?
7 Have we established key result areas and tasks for each job?
8 Does our appraisal system focus on improvable areas of performance?
9 Do we have a systematic approach to variance production, analysis and corrective action?
10 Should we use experiment and research more to test our hypotheses about the cause-effect relationships in the marketing activity?

A Systematic Programme for Reviewing and Improving Your Marketing Activity

It is well recognized that the most difficult task for the reader is to translate the facts, opinions and ideas from a book like this into effective action within the organization. This is why checklists have been provided at the end of each chapter to help act as a bridge from the inevitable generalities of the text to the specific problems and opportunities of the individual enterprise. The questions contained in those checklists are now repeated all together in the following pages but they have been regrouped to fit more precisely into the headings of the chart shown in Figure S.P.1. This diagram represents a total model of the marketing function and the key stages that need to be considered in depth.

If an overall review of the marketing activity is needed, it is suggested that a series of top management workshops could be held using the questions to provide outline agendas. Alternatively the questions and the concept diagram can be used to pinpoint specific parts of the marketing operation for deeper investigation whilst also indicating the prior elements on which the problem area depends and the successive activities that it affects. In addition to such total or partial audit and review purposes, we have also found this concept a useful starting point for the annual marketing planning process.

Finally having reviewed his marketing activity the Marketing Director should ponder the five key questions below, which have been extracted from Chapter 8. Only if he himself is effective can the marketing organization hope to progress and prosper in the future.

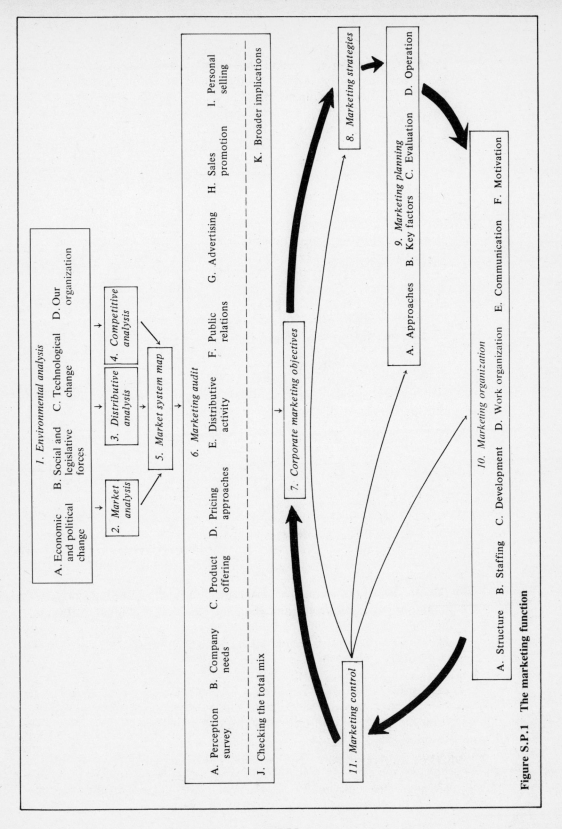

Figure S.P.1 The marketing function

1   Do I effectively measure and control the use of my time?
2   Do I focus my attention on results rather than activities?
3   Have I built the organization on its strengths?
4   Do I identify and concentrate attention on the few key areas where significant results can be obtained?
5   Do I make effective decisions?

1   Environmental analysis

A. Economic and political change
  i)   How is our cost structure being affected by national and international fluctuations?
 ii)   How are our markets being affected?
iii)   Is our pricing policy coping with inflation and currency rate instability?
iv)   Do we recognize the full implications of economic and political change on all the traditional bases of corporate policy?

B. Social and legislative forces
  i)   How are we reacting to consumerism?
 ii)   How are we affected by national and international legislation on products, prices, distribution and promotion?
iii)   Are we aware of the implications of employee legislation at home and abroad?

C. Technological change
  i)   What is the effect of technological change, especially in electronics, on our products or services?
 ii)   What is the effect on the consumers?
iii)   What is the effect on distributor activities?
iv)   What is the effect on our sales and marketing activities?

D. Our Organization
  i)   Do we accept the impact of economic/political, social/legislative and technology changes and their implications (e.g. globalization) on our business?
 ii)   Have we redefined our marketing philosophy in terms of strategic competitive differences?
iii)   Have we created a customer value driven culture throughout the enterprise?
iv)   Overall, are we capable of doing the 'simple' marketing things better than the competition to the increasing satisfaction of our customers?

2   Market analysis

  i)   How are the customer needs in which we are interested changing, especially in the ways in which they are satisfied?

  ii)   Is the total market changing in nature?
 iii) Is it changing in structure?
 iv) Is it changing in location?

3 Distributive analysis

   i)   How are the networks changing in nature?
  ii)   How are they changing in structure?
 iii) Have the factors affecting physical distribution changed?
 iv) How are international distribution patterns evolving?

4 Competitive analysis

   i)   How are our direct competitors changing?
  ii)   How are our indirect competitors changing?
 iii) Who are our potential competitors?
 iv) Could our customers become our competitors?

5 Market system map

   i)   Can we specify accurately our consumers' characteristics today?
  ii)   Have we reviewed our market segmentation criteria recently?
 iii) Have we an up-to-date understanding of the needs of our distributors and/or customers?
 iv) Have we a clear picture of the activities of direct and indirect competition?
  v)   Do we have sufficient qualitative as well as quantitative research data?

6 The marketing audit

A. The perception survey
   i)   Have we identified clearly enough the various groups we are aiming to satisfy (e.g. consumers, purchasers, distributors, customers, specifiers)?
  ii)   Have we checked objectively the satisfactions they require?
 iii) Do we know how well our total offering (i.e. the product/price/ promotion package) is currently satisfying their needs?
 iv) Do we know how well competitive offerings are satisfying those needs?

B. The needs of the company
   i)   Is there a clear definition of how the marketing activity should contribute to the profit mechanism of the firm?

ii) Does the marketing management team understand the financial mechanism?

iii) Are we using management ratios as a tool to diagnose the strengths and weaknesses of our financial performance?

iv) Do we compare our financial performance against other divisions or other companies to identify areas for improvement?

C. The present and future product offering

i) Do the current products match the current needs of the various groups in the market system cost-effectively?

ii) Do we know where they stand on their life cycles?

iii) Have we evaluated the product range recently?

iv) Is the product development process fully effective?

D. Pricing approach, policy and structure

i) Do we have a systematic approach to market-related pricing?

ii) Is our pricing fully up to date in the light of inflation, currency fluctuations, etc?

iii) Do we have a logical and up-to-date pricing structure?

iv) Are appropriate pricing strategies being used for different markets and/or product groups?

E. Distribution activity

i) Does our current distribution strategy give the desired market access and customer service levels?

ii) Have we considered deeply enough the changing balance of power *vis-á-vis* the distribution networks, outlets and competition?

iii) Are we supporting and controlling the outlets sufficiently?

iv) Is our physical distribution system kept in line with changing markets and company activities?

F. Public relations

i) With which target audiences should we be communicating?

ii) What are their levels of knowledge, attitude and opinion about the company?

iii) What do we want them to think and feel about the company?

iv) Do we check to see whether the PR activity has caused the desired changes in knowledge, attitude and opinion?

G. Advertising

i) Are the target audiences specified clearly?

ii) Are our messages likely to be persuasive?

iii) Is the agency properly briefed and controlled?

iv) Is the advertising measured against the communication objectives set for it?

H. Sales promotion

i) Have 'pressure points' been identified where sales promotion can be used effectively?

ii) Have specific promotion goals been set?
iii) Do the techniques selected match the goals?
iv) Are the promotions evaluated in terms of the overall mix objectives?

I. Personal selling
  i) How is the nature of the sales task changing?
 ii) Should other methods of contacting the customer (e.g. teleselling, van selling) be considered?
iii) Does the existing sales force have the appropriate knowledge and skill?
iv) Is the sales force appropriately structured and staffed?

J. Checking the total mix
  i) Does the total promotional activity cover every element in the market system?
 ii) Are the elements of the promotional mix congruent, integrated and synchronized?
iii) Is sufficient time, effort and money being spent on evaluation of the effectiveness of the mix in total and of each element?
iv) Do we have a solid basis for planning future promotional action?

K. Broader implications of the marketing audit
  i) Are we auditing early and regularly enough to allow adequate consideration of the key issues, not simply the current problems?
 ii) Do we know how accurately current management perceptions, attitudes and opinions reflect present realities?
iii) Are we improving our concepts and models of the market mechanism and its workings?
iv) Is the marketing activity inhibited by or inhibiting the effectiveness of the other functions of the organization?

7 Corporate marketing objectives

  i) Is there a detailed up-to-date analysis of what business(es) we are in?
 ii) Are there clear profit and profitability objectives broken down into goals for each component part of the business?
iii) Have growth rates been defined and is there an optimum rate and/or size beyond which we should not expand?
iv) Are the objectives practical, specific, where possible quantitative, timed, competitively advantageous and limited enough to ensure commitment?

8 Marketing strategies

  i) Have the four major categories of strategy - market penetration, market development, product development and diversification - been investigated in turn and thoroughly?

   ii)   Have the selected strategies been evaluated to ensure their relevance to the marketplace, the corporate objectives and resources, the marketing activity and the competitive situation?

  iii)   Have our strategies been checked and integrated into a cohesive approach which in turn could lead to redefinition or extension of our objectives?

  iv)   Do we have an effective mechanism for considering and deciding our corporate marketing direction?

9 Marketing planning

A. Approaches to marketing planning
    i)   Do we have a clear concept of the marketing planning activity specifying its goals and processes?
   ii)   Does our approach ensure that clear guidelines are given?
  iii)   Do we gain the advantages of both the corporate view and local experience?
  iv)   Is marketing planning well integrated with the other functional planning processes in the organization?
   v)   Are there sufficient opportunities for 'challenge' built into our approach?

B. Key factors for a successful marketing planning system
    i)   Does our system encourage creative and innovative planning?
   ii)   Do we have sufficiently standardized formats?
  iii)   Have all concerned in planning been given enough briefing and training?
  iv)   Have we reconsidered the time-spans for the plans recently?
   v)   Do we have a well constructed planning cycle?

C. Evaluating the marketing plan
    i)   How do we decide that there is sufficient action planned to achieve our objectives?
   ii)   Are our plans well integrated and synergistic?
  iii)   Is the timing synchronized and flexible where necessary?
  iv)   Are the actions and reactions of competition, distribution and even elements of our own company thoroughly considered?
   v)   Is the plan constructed so that it can be readily implemented and results evaluated against it?

D. Operating the marketing plan
    i)   Do we review performance against plan thoroughly and regularly enough?
   ii)   How do we ensure that our planning improves?
  iii)   Is planning seen as an essential, practical and integral part of the managerial function?
  iv)   Is the plan used to evaluate individual as well as corporate performance?

   v)   Overall, do we 'plan the work and work the plan' as effectively as we should?

10 Marketing organization

A. Structure
   i)   Do we fully understand how the current structure evolved?
   ii)   Have we defined all the tasks to be performed?
   iii)   Have we considered more cost-effective ways of performing them?
   iv)   Have we grouped the tasks of planning and implementation according to marketplace criteria?
   v)   Does the structure sufficiently reflect the particular opportunities and/or problems facing us?
   vi)   Have we established staffing levels on the basis of workload analysis?
   vii)   Is the marketing organization effectively integrated with other corporate activities, notably production and finance?

B. Key principles of staffing
   i)   Are all jobs clearly and concisely defined, with key results, key activities and evaluation criteria specified?
   ii)   Have person profiles been constructed identifying the key strengths that must be possessed?
   iii)   Have we considered complementary staffing in order to strengthen the team?
   iv)   Do we base placement decisions on predicted capability in the job to be filled rather than on performance in the current position?
   v)   Do we have a systematic recruitment and selection procedure which collects and verifies all relevant information?

C. Developing knowledge and skills
   i)   Do we conduct systematic training needs analyses?
   ii)   Do we fit the training to the individuals precisely enough?
   iii)   Do we relate training closely enough to the job?
   iv)   Have we explored all the training methods available?
   v)   Is our training and development programme sufficient to equip the marketing team for the future?

D. Organizing the work
   i)   Are our delegation processes effective and perceived to be so?
   ii)   Have we ensured that responsibility and authority are delegated together?
   iii)   Have we constructed systems for maintaining accountability?
   iv)   Have we reviewed all our meetings to ensure that they are necessary?
   v)   Are our meetings conducted effectively?

E. Establishing effective communications
   i)   Have we clearly defined our marketing management information needs?

ii)   Have we established systems which will provide the relevant data to the right persons quickly and accurately enough?
iii) Does communication flow smoothly up and down the marketing organization?
iv)   Does it flow smoothly across the marketing organization?
v)   Does the marketing organization have effective communication with the other company functions?

F. Motivating the marketing team
i)   Have we identified the prime motivational needs of our management and staff?
ii)   Have we a sound remuneration system?
iii) Do our people feel consulted, involved and committed both individually and as part of the team?
iv)   Do we provide enough opportunities for growth?
v)   Are we providing motivationally effective management?

11 Marketing control

i)   Have we defined the key areas of marketing activity that need to be evaluated?
ii)   Have we defined what is 'success' in each area?
iii) Have we identified the factors that will affect success in each area?
iv)   Have we established appropriate criteria for evaluating marketplace, distributive and corporate performance?
v)   Do we have a clear concept of the sequence of causal factors?
vi)   Does our management information system provide appropriate data to compare against the key criteria?
vii) Have we established key result areas and tasks for each job?
viii) Does our appraisal system focus on improvable areas of performance?
ix)   Do we have a systematic approach to variance production, analysis and corrective action?
x)   Should we use experiment and research more to test our hypotheses about the cause-effect relationships in the marketing activity?

Epilogue: Key Characteristics of the Successful Marketing Director

Many dozens of times throughout this book, the Marketing Director has been exhorted or encouraged to 'do this', 'ensure this', 'examine that'. It might appear that his task is too broad and complex for a normal human being! The job of the Marketing Director is certainly taxing, but all the observations made have been drawn from practical experience with top marketing management. As a final guide to Marketing Directors wishing to develop themselves, to General Managers wanting to understand the top marketing function better and perhaps more accurately select candidates for it, and to middle management aspiring to promotion, the key characteristics of successul Marketing Directors can be summarized as follows:

1 The Marketing Director must be knowledgeable about the major marketing methods and techniques. This implies an understanding of the eight major tactical areas of marketing: marketing research, product development, pricing, distribution, public relations, advertising, sales promotion and selling. Of course, it is unrealistic to expect the same level of expertise in each; in any case their relative importance varies according to the nature of the industry in which the company operates. However, without an understanding of all these areas, it is difficult to be certain that the right mix is being used.

Furthermore, not only must the Marketing Director be a jack of all the marketing trades; he needs to be master of some of them. Again, this will vary from industry to industry, but some elements are almost universally important. For example, there are few companies in any form of business where the Marketing Director does not need to be able to communicate personally and persuasively with major customers.

2   The Marketing Director must be effective as a manager, i.e. get things done through other people. He must know how to recruit, select, train, plan, organize and control marketing people and their activities. Much of this book has been concerned with this managerial dimension as it is the quality of the orchestration of resources which increasingly marks the difference between otherwise equally professional marketing organizations.

3   Perhaps most important, the Marketing Director must be able to function as a director. This implies being able to take a longer view than is necessary or even appropriate at operational management level, set long-term objectives, conceive strategically how they can be achieved and define a framework of targets, priorities and policies within which his management team can work effectively and enthusiastically. Furthermore, as a director, he must be capable of taking a corporate view of the business and not simply represent his own functional interests. He must have at least an understanding of the other major company activities, such as finance, production, research and development, in order to fulfill his own role as a member of the top management team.

Successful fulfilment of these three elements of the job demands a mix of knowledge, skill, experience and attitude. There is obviously a need for the Marketing Director to be knowledgeable about the marketing and managerial activities. Perhaps equally important is numeracy, especially in the financial area. Traditionally marketing has been a more qualitative than quantitative discipline, but there is now a significant trend towards the application of quantitative techniques which has been strengthened by the increasing availability of low-cost computing power. Furthermore as numbers are the only common language of all the functions of the business enterprise, numeracy is a key characteristic of Marketing Directors who are effective in their corporate top management roles.

   Of all the skills required, perhaps the most vital is communication ability, especially persuasive communication. The Marketing Director must be master of this if he is to lead his team, handle major customers and work with his colleagues on the board. It is rare to find a successful Marketing Director who lacks this skill; often is has been devloped in him at an early age through sales experience, which is still one of the most important areas of experience for any aspiring marketing man or woman to have.

   Of course, the Marketing Director will need to have had experience in more than the sales area if he is to be effective. Many successful Marketing Directors have added early to their sales expertise by working in marketing planning, product or brand management. Such jobs are particularly valuable as normally they encompass research, product development and promotion. Experience of two or more different marketing situations (which usually implies working for two or more companies) is often necessary to achieve the versatility demanded by many top marketing roles. Otherwise, it is difficult to understand how the relative importance of marketing tactics can change and how different mixes need to be constructed for varying marketing situations.

There is always the temptation for the one-company man to believe that the particular marketing approach that is effective in his circumstances represents the only marketing solution, or worse still that his situation is so different that experience from other industries does not apply. It is the hardening of such attitudes that causes industrial marketeers to believe that they have nothing to learn from consumer goods marketing and vice versa with both sides believing the other's task is not only simpler, but also requires less intelligence and expertise!

The successful Marketing Director has usually worked in sufficient different marketing situations to know that each has its own particular problems and solutions, but that much can be gained from the cross-application of experiences. Furthermore, such open-mindedness makes it easier to understand and use knowledge gained by others. As Bismarck said, 'It is only fools who learn from their own experiences; wise men learn from the experience of other people'.

The attitude with which the Marketing Director uses his knowledge, skill and experience can determine the degree of his success. Most effective Marketing Directors tend to take what might be termed as a scientific approach to the job. Systematically, they identify the problems and opportunities, collect data, formulate solutions, where necessary test them, cause them to be implemented and evaluate the results. Throughout this continuously repeated process, they remain as objective as possible, prepared to discard faulty solutions even when the original idea was their own, and always recognizing that a successful initiative in one situation is no guarantee of a universal solution. In a fast changing world, problems and their solutions change equally rapidly.

Finally, the attitude of Marketing Directors to their corporate role is balanced between the responsibility of heading the marketing function and the overall health of the organization. Thus they should recognize that although their functional marketing objectives are important, there are times when they may have to be modified, perhaps severely, in the light of corporate needs.

This profile of the key characteristics of successful Marketing Directors may seem idealized; it is perhaps expecting too much of any person to be outstanding in all the aspects discussed. However, in an increasingly competitive and volatile world, the quality of the performance of the Marketing Director is vital to the current health and future prosperity of any enterprise. As prime guardian of the marketing concept, he must help guide the organization to the fulfilment of its major purpose, satisfying consumer needs better than the competition and at a profit for his company and its shareholders.

Booklist

General

Baker, M.J. (ed.), *The Marketing Book,* Heinemann, 1987.
Bonoma, T.V., *The Marketing Edge,* The Free Press, 1985.
Drucker, P., *Managing for Results,* Pan Books, 1967.
Goldsmith, W. and Clutterbuck, D., *The Winning Streak,* Penguin, 1984.
Kotler, P., *Marketing Management,* Prentice-Hall, 1984.
Levitt, T., *Innovation in Marketing,* Pan Books, 1968.
McBurnie, T. and Clutterbuck, D., *The Marketing Edge,* Weidenfeld and Nicholson, 1987.
Morse, S.P., *Practical Approach to Marketing Management,* McGraw-Hill, 1967.
Peters, J.T. and Austin, N., *A Passion for Excellence,* Collins, 1985.
Peters, J.T. and Waterman, R.H., *In Search of Excellence,* Harper & Row, 1982.
Porter, M.E., *Competitive Advantage,* The Free Press, 1985.
Porter, M.E., *Competitive Strategy,* The Free Press, 1980.

Chapter 1

Robertson, A., *Strategic Marketing - A Business Response to Consumerism,* Associated Business Press, 1978.
Toffler, A., *Future Shock,* Bodley Head, 1970, Pan Books, 1973.

Chapter 2

Chisnall, P.M., *Marketing - A Behavioural Analysis,* McGraw-Hill, 1985.

Guirdham, M., *Marketing - The Management of Distribution Channels*, Pergamon, 1972.
Melkman, A.V., *How to Handle Major Customers Profitably*, Gower, 1979.

Chapter 3

Baker, M.J. and McTavish, R., *Product Policy and Management*, Macmillan, 1976.
Gabor, A., *Pricing:Principles and Practice*, Gower, 2nd edition, 1988.
Naylor, J. and Wood, A., *Practical Marketing Audits*, Associated Business Press, 1978.
Pike, C.K., *Financial Glossary - A Checklist*, Marketing Improvements Limited, 1979.

Chapter 4

Aaker, D.A. and Myers, J.G., *Advertising Management*, Prentice-Hill, 1975.
Wilson, M.T., *Managing a Sales Force*, Gower, 2nd edition, 1983.
Marketing Improvements Limited (ed), *Sales Management Handbook*, Gower, 1988.
Marketing Improvements Limited, *Sales Planner*, Gower, 1988.

Chapter 5

Adler, L., *Plotting Marketing Strategy*, Business Books.
Ansoff, I., *Corporate Strategy*, Sidgwick & Jackson Ltd, 1986.

Chapter 6

Miller, E.C., *Marketing Planning*, American Management Association.
Stapleton, J., *How to Prepare a Marketing Plan*, Gower, 4th edition, 1988.

Chapter 7

O'Shaughnessy, J., *Patterns of Business Organisation*, Allen and Unwin, 1976.

Chapter 8

Drucker, P., *The Effective Executive*, Heinemann, 1967, Pan Books, 1970.
Lidstone, J., *How to Recruit and Select Successful Salesmen*, Gower, 1983.

Chapter 9

Herzberg, F., *Work and the Nature of Man,* Crosby Lockwood, 1975.
Humble, J., *Improving Business Results,* McGraw-Hill, 1982.
Lidstone, J., *Motivating Your Sales Force,* Gower, 1978.

Chapter 10

Johnson, A.S., *Marketing and Financial Control,* Pergamon, 1967.

Index